Celebrities
with
Heart

Angelina Jolie

Celebrity with Heart

Michael A. Schuman

Enslow Publishers, Inc.
40 Industrial Road
Box 398
Berkeley Heights, NJ 07922
USA

http://www.enslow.com

To Trisha and Allie, on their way to becoming exemplary role models.

Library of Congress Cataloging-in-Publication Data

Schuman, Michael.
    Angelina Jolie : celebrity with heart / Michael A. Schuman.
        p. cm. — (Celebrities with heart)
    Summary: "A biography of American actress and philanthropist Angelina Jolie"—
        Provided by publisher.
    Includes bibliographical references and index.
    ISBN-13: 978-0-7660-3403-7
    1. Jolie, Angelina, 1975—Juvenile literature. 2. Motion picture actors and actresses—
        United States—Biography—Juvenile literature. I. Title.
    PN2287.J583S38 2010
    791.4302'8092—dc22
    [B]
                                                    2009023807

ISBN-13: 978-1-59845-203-7 (paperback)

Printed in the United States of America

052010 Lake Book Manufacturing, Inc., Melrose Park, IL

10 9 8 7 6 5 4 3 2 1

To Our Readers: We have done our best to make sure all Internet Addresses in this book were active and appropriate when we went to press. However, the author and the publisher have no control over and assume no liability for the material available on those Internet sites or on other Web sites they may link to. Any comments or suggestions can be sent by e-mail to comments@enslow.com or to the address on the back cover.

Every effort has been made to locate all copyright holders of material used in this book. If any errors or omissions have occurred, corrections will be made in future editions of this book. This book has not been authorized by Angelina Jolie.

♻ Enslow Publishers, Inc., is committed to printing our books on recycled paper. The paper in every book contains 10% to 30% post-consumer waste (PCW). The cover board on the outside of each book contains 100% PCW. Our goal is to do our part to help young people and the environment too!

Illustration Credits: Associated Press/Wide World Photos, pp. 7, 12, 49, 58, 63, 70, 74, 88, 99, 104; Everett Collection, Inc., pp. 4, 15, 22, 26, 32, 38, 44, 47, 78, 85; Getty Images, p. 1.

Cover Illustration: Getty Images

Contents

Angelina Jolie portrays Lara Croft in a scene from Lara Croft: Tomb Raider.

Land Mines and Lara Croft

When actor Angelina Jolie was filming *Lara Croft: Tomb Raider* in Cambodia in 2000, she had some time to see the country. Civil war had raged throughout much of Cambodia in the 1970s. Weapons had included land mines, which are explosive devices placed just below ground. They explode when a person or vehicle makes contact with them. People either die or suffer hideous injuries as a result. Jolie discovered that long after the fighting ended, land mines still exist in Cambodia. The film crew's movement had been restricted because of these weapons. After touring Cambodia, Jolie said, "I was shocked by the amount of land mines and all the landmine victims."[1]

Jolie wanted to do something to help, but did not know where to turn. She decided to contact the United Nations (UN). The UN is an organization made up of most of the world's nations. The UN's main purpose is for nations to get together and discuss and solve disputes. Unfortunately, not all conflicts can be resolved peacefully.

However, the UN sponsors several smaller groups that do good works. One is the United Nations High Commissioner for Refugees (UNHCR). Its main goal is to help war refugees—people who have to flee their native land as a result of war. They are often forgotten war victims. The UNHCR attends to refugees' basic needs by providing them with food, water, and medicine. When it is safe, the UNHCR helps refugees return to their homes. If it is not safe, the UNHCR helps refugees find homes in neutral countries.

Jolie contacted the UNHCR and said she wanted to help refugees and landmine victims like she had seen in Cambodia. It helped that she is a famous actor. The entertainment media would discuss her work with the UNHCR as well as her lifestyle or romantic life. Fans and others interested in Jolie would then become aware of the problems of land mines and refugees. When asked what drew her to Cambodia, Jolie responded, "I think it's a lot of things like knowing the history of a place, [and] having not been taught [it] at school. I felt I should

Angelina Jolie smiles during a ceremony at the headquarters of the United Nations High Commissioner for Refugees (UNHCR) in Geneva, Switzerland on August 27, 2001. Jolie was named the agency's goodwill ambassador at the ceremony.

have been taught about the landmine problem. It made me suddenly realize certain things about the world and how much I had to learn, like the history of the people."[2]

Within weeks of contacting the UNHCR, the group allowed Jolie to take a goodwill trip to a troubled land far away. It was not Cambodia, but another area wracked by civil war: the African nations of Sierra Leone and Tanzania. Her goals were to learn how she could help refugees and to make others aware of their problems.

Jolie's father, actor Jon Voight, knew his daughter was heading to a dangerous place. He tried to get her to cancel her trip. Jolie wrote, "I was angry with him, but I told him I know he loves me and that as my father he was trying to protect me from harm. We embraced and smiled at one another."[3] Her then-husband, actor Billy Bob Thornton, and their friends did not understand why she felt she had to travel to help out. They believed she could publicize landmine problems and send relief money without leaving the comforts of home. Thornton asked her, "Why are you going to do these things? What do you think you can possibly accomplish?"[4] She answered that she could not fully understand a place's problems without being there. She went ahead and made the trip. Soon, humanitarian causes became a second career for Jolie.

2

"Come On, Angie, Give Us a Show!"

Angelina Jolie was born on June 4, 1975, in Los Angeles, California. Her real name is Angelina Jolie Voight. *Angelina* means "pretty little angel" in Italian. Her parents called her by the nickname Angie.

Jolie's father, Jon Voight, began making hit movies in the late 1960s. More recently he played Mr. Sir in the 2003 movie *Holes*, starring Shia LeBoeuf.

Voight married a young actress named Marcheline Bertrand in 1971. Because her name sounds French, Bertrand (whose birth name was Marcia Lynne) was often mistaken for an actress from Paris. Jolie emphasized that is not true. She stated, "My mother is as far from French Parisian as you can get. . . . She's part Iroquois Indian, from Chicago. She grew up in a bowling alley that my grandparents owned."[1]

Angie's father later said that there is no Iroquois ancestry in Marcheline's heritage. Voight admitted he and Marcheline made it up to make his wife's background seem more exotic. He said, "We always liked the idea of her as an Iroquois, and I love that my kids have picked up on that."[2]

The couple had a son in 1973. He was named James Haven Voight. After James's birth, Bertrand devoted her life to being a mother. By the time Angelina was born in 1975, Bertrand had given up her dreams of acting. Being a mother of two small children was tough. It was especially difficult considering that her husband was often away from their Los Angeles home filming movies.

Before Angie was a year old, her father decided he no longer wanted to be married. Voight left his family, leaving Bertrand to raise two preschool children on her own. Although Voight was no longer part of Bertrand's life, the two did not divorce until 1978.

Los Angeles has for years had a bad smog problem, which can take a toll on people's breathing ability. Because the smog was affecting Bertrand's health, she took her two children and settled in a place with cleaner air: Palisades, New York. Palisades is a quiet town about twenty-five miles north of bustling New York City. Moving to a new home did not affect Angie's happiness. Like many little girls, she liked to play dress-up. She pranced around her house in plastic high heel shoes. She enjoyed putting on tassels and sparkly decorations. Angie remembers bouncing on her bed with her brother to a Mousercize video. She loved the character Mr. Spock from the television show *Star Trek*, and one of her favorite movies was *Dumbo*.

Angie had an active imagination, and invented theater-style games with her friends. She loved to be the center of attention. Her brother would point a video camera in her direction. Then he would call out, "Come on, Angie, give us a show!"[3] She would then perform a little skit. She usually wore her own costumes that were lovingly made by her mother. Angie was delighted when she made people laugh. James remembered Angie acting as if she was in a commercial for Subway restaurants. She would jokingly say into the camera, "I'll punch your face if you don't buy a sandwich."[4]

Although her father had left the family, he still stayed in touch with them. Voight by then had become one of the world's most respected actors. In 1978 he won an Academy Award, or Oscar, for best actor in a motion picture. He earned it for playing a paralyzed Vietnam War veteran in the movie *Coming Home*.

Angelina Jolie with her mother Marcheline Bertrand at a film premiere in July 2001.

The next year, Voight starred in *The Champ*. He plays a boxer named Billy, who dies from boxing injuries soon after winning a title match. When six-year-old James and four-year-old Angie watched the movie, they found it troubling. Angie especially had a problem separating her real father from the role he played. When Billy died on screen, Angie thought her father had really died. "I freaked out," she recalled.[5] Voight realized Angie was upset. He said of his children, "They both started weeping. The last scene was very unsettling. I had to take them in my arms and explain that Daddy was just acting— that he wasn't dead, that he was still here with them."[6]

In 1982, Voight decided to put Angie in one of his movies. It was a comedy Voight co-wrote entitled *Lookin' to Get Out*. Voight plays a crooked gambler. Angie plays Tosh, the daughter of his ex-girlfriend. In her one scene, Tosh meets her father for the first time. She wears a flower-print dress and a straw hat. Angie folds her hands in front of her. She sees that her father's arm is in a sling. Angie fidgets a little as she asks if he is okay. He replies that he was hurt because he crossed the street against the light. He tells her in a nice way never to do that. She tells him he is a nice man. Although she was on screen for just a few minutes, her father said, "She was fantastic. She stole the scene, of course."[7] Her father saw Angie's movie debut differently than her fans did. Voight saw it as a chance to reunite with his family. Although he was divorced from Marcheline Bertrand, he also gave her a small part, too. Voight commented, "It was wonderful just to be working with my kids and to all be together at that moment."[8]

Lookin' to Get Out did not make Angie a star. The movie received poor reviews. Respected movie critic Richard Corliss from *Time* magazine called the movie "a sloppy mess."[9] Except for the fact that it was Angelina Jolie's first movie appearance, *Lookin' to Get Out* is forgettable. However, many diehard fans have bought the DVD just so they can have a complete collection of Angelina Jolie films.

It was several years before Angie appeared in another movie. But she did love going to movies as a child. Her favorite companion was her mother. Even though Angie's father was a real-life famous actor, she credits all those movie dates with her mother for giving her an interest in acting.[10]

In elementary school, Angie was part of a group called the Kissy Girls. They would chase boys until they captured them. Then they would kiss the boys until they screamed. When school officials found out about them, they called the girls' parents and that put an end to the Kissy Girls.

With her love of frilly, feminine clothing and being a member of the Kissy Girls, Angie seemed to be a real girly girl. But Angie stood apart from the rest of the girls in her choice of pets. She did not prefer kittens or puppies. Angie's pets were snakes and lizards. She named her favorite lizard Vladimir. She called her snake Harry Dean Stanton, after the well-known actor. She said that one reason she likes snakes is that most people do not like them.

A six-year-old Angelina Jolie makes her screen debut opposite her father Jon Voight and Ann-Margaret in the 1982 film *Lookin' to Get Out*.

When Angie was eleven, her mother moved their family back to the West Coast. They settled in Beverly Hills, next to Los Angeles. When many people hear the name "Beverly Hills," they think of rich people driving fancy cars and living in mansions. Certainly, a large number of wealthy families live in Beverly Hills. However, there are many residents of Beverly Hills from more modest backgrounds.

Even though Angie's father made good money as an actor, the family relied mainly on income from Marcheline's odd jobs. Angie's family was not poor. But compared to some of Angie's wealthy classmates, she stood out. While some of Angie's classmates lived in big houses, Marcheline moved from one basic apartment to another. Angie's classmates showed up at school in the trendiest clothes, but Angie wore secondhand clothing. Voight refused to spoil his children. He always maintained that his children should learn to appreciate the value of money.

Some of the students from richer families made fun of Angie for wearing old clothes that did not fit properly. In addition, Angie wore eyeglasses. For a while, she had braces on her teeth. Kids picked on her for that, too. They teased her about her full lips and skinny figure. Simply put, Angie did not fit in. Those school years were tough for her. She managed to cope by developing a close bond with her mother. Because her mother struggled with money and Angie with self-esteem, Angie said that she and her mother shared an "us against the world" attitude.[11]

Despite her school problems, Angie never lost interest in acting. Outside school, she enrolled in classes at a famous acting academy called the Lee Strasberg Theatre Institute. The institute has branches in both New York City and Los Angeles. Lee Strasberg was an actor, a director, and a producer. In 1969 he began his school to teach talented actors how to polish their skills.

> Angie said that she and her mother shared an "us against the world" attitude.

Strasberg taught a technique called "method acting." In method acting, actors try to constantly feel the emotions of their characters. The actors may be asked to dig into their own memories and relive some of their worst experiences to understand what their characters are going through. Even off camera, many try to stay in character. Some of the world's greatest actors sharpened their talents at the Strasberg Institute. These include Al Pacino, Robert De Niro, Paul Newman, Jane Fonda, and Marilyn Monroe.

Angie left public school and studied at the Strasberg Institute for two years. She acted in several of the institute's productions. However, she quit because she said she did not have enough memories in her young life to properly portray her characters. She returned to public school.

Cyborgs and Computer Hackers

When she returned to school, Angie was no happier at Beverly Hills High than she had been two years earlier. Because she was still not seen as pretty and because of her modest home life, Angie felt like an outcast.[1] She said, "Thirteen, fourteen [years old], that was a bad time."[2]

By now, she was experimenting with drugs. She collected knives and coped with her unhappy life by cutting herself on a regular basis. Jolie confessed, "For some reason, the ritual of having cut myself and feeling . . . the pain, maybe, feeling alive, feeling some kind of release, it was somehow therapeutic to me."[3]

She described those days by saying. "I was always that punk in school. . . . I didn't feel clean [or] pretty."[4]

She soon started dressing the part. Angie dyed her hair purple. She wore black boots, ripped jeans, and grungy jackets. Other times she dressed in leather. She filled her school notebooks with pictures of daggers and other knives. In between the drawings were comments about death and dying.[5] Angie dreamed of becoming a funeral director. She actually ordered a copy of the *Funeral Service Institute Handbook*, and answered the test questions inside.

A classmate named Jean Robinson recalled, "I don't think there had ever been anybody quite like her at Beverly Hills High."[6]

At age fourteen Angie had a boyfriend who was a kindred spirit. He was sixteen years old and into the punk lifestyle too. They spent their nights hanging around punk music clubs in some of the toughest areas of Los Angeles. She and her boyfriend experimented with cutting each other. Today Angie has a faint scar on her jawline from when her boyfriend cut her there.

Angie soon lost interest in school and dropped out. She later confessed, "I think now that if somebody would have taken me at 14 and dropped me in the middle of Asia or Africa, I'd have realized how self-centered I was, and that there was real pain and real death—real things to fight for, so that I wouldn't have been fighting myself so much. I wish, when I was thinking about suicide, I'd have seen how many people are dying each day that have no choice in the matter. I would have appreciated the fact that I had a choice."[7]

The most Angie's mother could do was try to protect her. She could have forbidden Angie from seeing her boyfriend. But Marcheline knew that might drive the couple closer together. Instead, she decided to keep Angie close by, where she could watch her. She allowed Angie's boyfriend to move into their home.

It was a bizarre situation, but it worked. There were scary times, though. Angie once sliced her body so badly that she almost cut her jugular vein, a large vein in the neck that draws blood from one's head. A cut in the jugular can be fatal. She was rushed to the hospital. Angie then decided she had had enough of the self-cutting and the punk scene. She split up with her boyfriend and moved into her own apartment near her mother's home.

Even with all her wild behavior, Angie never lost her love for acting. She returned to Beverly Hills High School and graduated at sixteen. Most high school students do not graduate until they are seventeen or eighteen. Although she had spent two very valuable years at the Strasberg Institute, by now she was taking acting lessons from her own private coach: her father.

Angelina and her brother James with their father Jon Voight at the 1988 Academy Awards.

She visited her dad regularly. They would run through plays together, with the two playing different roles. Every Sunday they would get together and do an entire play. Jon gave his daughter advice based on his years of experience. He said, "I gave her what help I could in terms of acting, but she went out and made a career of her own."[8]

Angie's brother, James, went on to college. He studied filmmaking at the University of Southern California (USC) in Los Angeles. Angie tried modeling. By sixteen years old she had developed more confidence in her looks. She no longer wore braces and had switched from glasses to contact lenses. She was hired by an agency called Finesse Model Management. Angie had several modeling gigs in Los Angeles. Other modeling jobs took her to New York City and London, England. It was an exciting life for a teenage girl.

One side benefit of her modeling work was the chance to appear in music videos. In the early 1990s the cable television network MTV presented music videos almost twenty-four hours a day. The videos provided opportunities for young models and actors to gain experience in a new form of acting. They spoke no lines in music videos, but had to act out stories that accompanied the songs.

Angie appeared in several, including some for big names such as "Rock 'n' Roll Dreams Come Through" by Meat Loaf, "Anybody Seen My Baby" by the Rolling Stones, and "Stand By My Woman" by Lenny Kravitz. She also fine-tuned her acting skills by appearing in five student films directed by her brother.

Most young actors have to try out, or audition, for a play before they are hired. Angie was still a teenager when she auditioned for a role in *Room Service*. There are two main female characters in the play. Those would seem to be the obvious choices for a young female actor. However, it was not like Angelina Jolie to do the obvious. She tried out for the role of Gregory Wagner, a blustery, middle-aged hotel owner. As the name indicates, the part is usually played by a man. But Angie got the part and played it as a woman.

Her father said he was stunned when he went to see the play and saw Angie on stage in the role of Wagner. But when he stopped to consider what he was watching, Voight exclaimed, "Oh my God, she's just like me. She'll take these crazy parts and be thrilled that she can make people chuckle or whatever."[9]

Due to her modeling and acting in small plays, Angie was becoming well known in the inner circles of the movie and theater industry. But it was not because of her famous last name. Around this time she dropped the name Voight. She became known simply as Angelina

Jolie. She explained, "I dropped my name because it was important that I was my own person."[10]

She was offered a chance to appear in her first full-length movie since she appeared in that short scene with her father in *Lookin' to Get Out* about a decade earlier. The movie was *Cyborg 2: Glass Shadow*. It was a sequel to the 1989 movie *Cyborg*, a science-fiction thriller set in the future. In the movie, Earth has become a dismal place and the main character, played by Belgian actor Jean-Claude Van Damme, tries to stop a killer plague. The cure lies inside the brain of a cyborg—a being that is half human and half robot.

The original *Cyborg* received mostly poor reviews. One of the best-known movie critics, Roger Ebert, wrote that the lines were so bad they were "unspeakable."[11] Despite the critics' pans, *Cyborg* developed a following among sci-fi fans. It made money for the studio and launched Van Damme's career as an action star.

However, Van Damme did not appear in *Cyborg 2: Glass Shadow*. The movie was shot on a small budget. It never played in movie theaters and was released straight to video.

Like *Cyborg*, *Cyborg 2: Glass Shadow* received negative reviews. Unlike *Cyborg*, it did not earn much money. Jolie played the role of a female cyborg, Cash Reese. Cash has been programmed to destroy a rival cyborg factory

A movie poster for *Cyborg 2: Glass Shadow*, one of Angelina's earliest breaks into acting as an adult.

designed to turn human beings into their slaves. However, the human side of Cash triumphs when she falls in love with a human combat instructor.

Jolie was not pleased by the movie or her performance. In fact, after she first saw it she went home to her mother's apartment and got physically sick.[12] Her brother, James, was there and he did his best to make her feel better.

The poor reviews by critics also bothered her. Jolie noted that it is easy for actors to judge their self-worth based on what critics say. She stated, "If you have enough people sitting around telling you you're wonderful, then you start believing you're fabulous. Then someone tells you you stink, and you believe that too."[13]

Though discouraged, Jolie did not give up. She was given a small part in the 1995 crime drama *Without Evidence*. It was seen by very few moviegoers and was also panned by critics. However, her next movie, *Hackers*, would affect Jolie both personally and professionally. It was a different kind of role for Jolie and it made more people notice her talents.

Award-Winning Angie

*H*ackers starred young actors who had never been in a hit movie. It also featured an ensemble cast. Most movies have one or two lead actors and some supporting actors. Supporting actors play roles that are important to the plot, but not as important as the leads. In an ensemble movie, several actors have equally important roles in relation to the plot.

One character in *Hackers* is Dade Murphy, a computer genius. He was played by twenty-two-year old British actor Jonny Lee Miller. When the character of Dade was eleven, he hacked into computers operated by the United States stock market. He was caught after causing a huge financial crisis. As punishment, he was ordered never to go near a computer until he turned eighteen years old. When the movie starts, he is eighteen.

Another character is Kate Libby, played by Jolie. Kate is one of Dade's classmates. Kate and Dade do not get along at first. Over the course of the movie, they gradually start liking each other. By the movie's end, the two are a romantic couple.

The actors spent several weeks learning how computers work. They also had to learn in-line skating since Kate and Dade spend time racing on them. As they prepared for their roles, Miller and Jolie found themselves taking the same paths as their characters. They were falling in love.

Hackers came out in September 1995. The movie did not make much money and most critics did not like it. Movie reviewer David Kronke was typical. He said the characters looked too slick to be computer hackers and it took too long for the plot to be established. He cleverly wrote, "This movie megabytes."[1]

Another reviewer who did not like the movie was Hal Hinson of the *Washington Post*. Hinson even made fun of Jolie's full lips, just as the girls in her school used to. Hinson wrote, that Jolie's "lips are so pouty and bee-stung that they seem about to explode."[2]

However, some critics liked *Hackers*. Roger Ebert was one. He said *Hackers* was "well directed, written and acted."[3] Ebert had especially kind words for Jolie and Miller. He wrote, "Jolie, the daughter of Jon Voight, and Miller, a British newcomer, bring a particular quality to their performances that is convincing and engaging."[4] Another reviewer who liked the movie was Joe Leydon of *Variety*, a show business newspaper. Leydon wrote, "Miller and Jolie are appropriately engaging as the romantic leads."[5]

While *Hackers* was not a hit, it did give Jolie's career a boost. Jolie would make many movies over the next several years.

Meanwhile, in March 1996, Jolie and Miller were married. Miller was twenty-three years old. Jolie was a few months short of her twenty-first birthday. They kept their wedding small—so small that there were only two guests. Miller did not meet his bride's famous father until weeks after the couple was married. Neither bride nor groom wore traditional wedding attire. Instead of a tuxedo or other kind of formal wear, Miller dressed in leather. Jolie wore a white shirt and black rubber pants. On her shirt she wrote her husband's name in her blood.

Miller and Jolie both got tattoos for the occasion. Miller had a pet snake, so he had a snake tattooed on his wrist. Jolie had a tattoo representing bravery drawn on her arm and one representing death on her shoulder.

The couple settled in Los Angeles and Jolie got busy making one movie after another. In 1996 alone, three movies featuring Jolie were released. The first was the romantic comedy *Mojave Moon.* Jolie plays Eleanor Rigby, also the title of a famous Beatles song. Known by the nickname Elie, she wants to visit her mother who lives in a trailer in California's Mojave Desert. She gets a ride from Al McCord, a much-older car salesman. Elie finds herself falling in love with Al while Al falls in love with Elie's mother. *Mojave Moon* did not play for long in theaters but is shown on cable television now and then.

The same can be said for her next 1996 movie, *Love Is All There Is.* It is a modern-day version of Shakespeare's *Romeo and Juliet.* In the movie, two Italian-American families in the Bronx are having a feud. As in *Romeo and Juliet,* one daughter, played by Jolie, falls in love with a son from the other family. *Love Is All There Is* had its share of fans, but also did not catch on with a wide audience.

The other Jolie movie from 1996 was the drama *Foxfire.* In the movie, a group of schoolgirls take revenge on a teacher who sexually harasses them. It is based on a novel by the writer Joyce Carol Oates. However, Oates's novel takes place in the 1950s. The setting for the movie

Jonny Lee Miller and Angelina Jolie in a scene from *Hackers*.

is the 1990s. Most critics panned the movie, saying that changing the setting did not work.

Again, Jolie found herself in love with a costar. Her name was Jenny Shimizu, a model and female actor. Because she was now dating a woman, Jolie was getting a reputation as a wild woman who liked to experiment. Jolie and Miller were still married, but because of their filming schedules, they spent little time together. Even when living in the same city, married actors might rarely see each other since workdays lasting up to twelve hours are common. It can take hours to set up and film a single scene that might last just a few minutes in a finished movie.

At this time Jolie was seriously concentrating on her career. She said, "It's not fair to the other person that I'm so busy with my career and that I'm often distant even when I am with someone."[6] She added, "We were living side by side, but we had separate lives."[7]

A feature movie she made in 1997 was titled *Playing God.* It was a dark comedy, a movie that makes light of serious issues. Jolie played a gangster's girlfriend. Like her previous movies, *Playing God* received mostly poor reviews from professional critics. Edward Guthmann, movie critic for the *San Francisco Chronicle,* went so far as to call the movie "a piece of garbage."[8] And Liam Lacey, critic for the Canadian newspaper the *Toronto*

Globe and Mail, criticized Jolie's looks. He said she is "sultry, dark-eyed [and] fat-lipped."[9] Once more, she started dating a costar. This time it was actor Timothy Hutton, who played the gangster.

Jolie finally received the attention she deserved when she decided to make movies for a different audience. These movies were not shown in theaters. They were made for television. A lot of actors choose not to appear in made-for-television movies. They think it is beneath their status as actors. But Jolie was not bothered by that.[10]

The first of her television movies was a western, *True Women.* It first ran as a miniseries on the CBS television network in May 1997, being televised over two consecutive days. *True Women* stars Dana Delaney as Sarah McClure, a pioneer woman in nineteenth-century Texas, whose strength is tested time and time again. Jolie plays her best friend, Georgina Virginia Lawshe Woods. Georgina and Sarah go through similar difficult experiences. At one point Georgina is forced to put on a brave face as she sings her dying child to sleep.

Jolie's next role in a movie made for television was a true departure. The movie was a docudrama, or a scripted drama based on a true story, about former Alabama governor George Wallace. Wallace supported segregation, or separation of African Americans and white people. Segregation had been common throughout the South. Wallace fought hard in the early 1960s to keep segregation legal in his state. That stand made him a popular governor in Alabama.

Wallace ran for President of the United States four times, although he never won. In 1972, he was shot in an assassination attempt by a disturbed young man named Arthur Bremer. Wallace was paralyzed and spent the rest of his life in a wheelchair. In his last term as governor, from 1983 to 1987, Wallace appeared to have a change of heart regarding race relations. He appointed African Americans to state government positions. He also publicly apologized for his past views supporting segregation. Some analysts said that after spending ten years in a wheelchair, he could now understand people who had suffered.

Jolie played Wallace's second wife, Cornelia. It might seem a stretch for an actor raised in New York and Los Angeles to play a southern governor's wife. Yet Jolie showed her versatility by speaking with a strong southern accent and sounding convincing.

She was so convincing that she was nominated for both an Emmy Award and a Golden Globe Award for her acting talents. Emmy Awards are given for excellence in television by the Academy of Television Arts & Sciences (ATAS). Its members are people who work in television, from actors to technicians. Golden Globe

Awards are given for excellence in both television and movies by the Hollywood Foreign Press Association (HFPA). The HFPA consists of journalists who cover American entertainment for publications based in other countries.

Jolie missed out on the Emmy, but won the Golden Globe. She finally earned some respect as an actor. The movie's director was John Frankenheimer, who in his long career directed classic movies such as *The Manchurian Candidate* and *Birdman of Alcatraz*. Frankenheimer praised Jolie, saying, "The world is full of beautiful girls. . . . But they're not Angelina Jolie. She's fun, honest, intelligent, gorgeous and divinely talented."[11]

"The world is full of beautiful girls. . . . But they're not Angelina Jolie."

Now movie critics began to accept what Frankenheimer knew and what Jolie's fans had realized for years. She is a very attractive woman. Instead of criticizing her full lips, they began to openly admire them.[12]

That respect was underlined when she won a second Golden Globe Award the next year. She received it for acting in a lead role in *Gia*, a movie made for the HBO cable television network. *Gia* is a powerful but a tragic story. Like *George Wallace,* it is based on the life of a real person, Gia Carangi, one of the most successful fashion models in the early 1980s. Gia was a tough woman who collected knives and had an in-your-face attitude. She dazzled people with her looks. It seemed like Jolie was born to play *Gia*.

At the peak of her success, Gia had money and fame. She could have had anything she wanted, but she ruined her life by becoming addicted to hard drugs. Even after going through a drug rehabilitation program, there was more tragedy in her life. She contracted AIDS.

AIDS is a name for a group of infections resulting from damage to the human immune system. AIDS stands for Acquired Immune Deficiency Syndrome. It is spread through direct contact with the HIV virus in an infected person's blood or other bodily fluids. Gia contracted AIDS by using an infected needle while injecting herself with the addictive drug, heroin. Today it is well known that sharing needles increases the risk of contracting AIDS. But not much was known about AIDS at the time.

Jolie showed a broad range of intense emotions playing Gia. She had to express rage, sadness, and sheer joy. Jolie used techniques she learned at the Strasberg Institute. Even when not working on the movie she stayed in character. When Gia suffered from the killing effects of the AIDS virus, she lost much of her hair.

Jolie as the model Gia in the eponymous 1998 HBO movie.

Some actors would simply wear a bald hairpiece, but Jolie actually shaved her head for the role.

After *Gia,* Jolie decided to learn about other aspects of making movies. She moved across the country to attend filmmaking classes at New York University in New York City. These were not acting classes. They were classes in directing and writing screenplays. But Jolie soon realized those parts of the cinematic arts were not for her. She made up her mind that she should be acting in movies, not writing or directing them.

So she moved back to Los Angeles and appeared in five movies in little over a year. Two were released in 1998. One was *Hell's Kitchen,* a crime drama about a botched robbery. Critics had mixed feelings about *Hell's Kitchen.* Her second 1998 release, *Playing by Heart,* is an ensemble movie focusing on the lives of eleven single people looking for love. *Playing by Heart* is what is often referred to as a sleeper. It received mostly positive reviews, but for some reason never caught on with the public. James Berardinelli of the Web site *Reelviews* raved about Jolie's acting: "Angelina Jolie, who gives the film's standout performance, is luminous."[13]

In the winter of 1999, Jolie had more on her mind than movies. She and her husband Jonny Lee Miller had drifted further apart. He moved back to London. He explained, "I know this sounds mad, but I was missing little things like the Nine O'clock News, red buses, country smells, the sound of our rock music and Match of the Day."[14]

Jolie put much of the blame on herself. She said that she put in so many hours on her job that they did not have time to make the marriage work.[15] Despite the divorce, she said that she and Miller remained good friends.[16] However, Jolie would not be single much longer.

Winning the Big One

Jolie's next movie, *Pushing Tin,* is a comedy-drama about air traffic controllers. It is yet another ensemble movie. Jolie plays Mary Bell, an air traffic controller's wife. Her husband, Russell, is played by actor and Oscar winner Billy Bob Thornton.

Thornton and Jolie happened to share the same manager, Geyer Kosinski. A manager helps guide an actor's career. Kosinski told both Thornton and Jolie about each other. He thought they had a lot in common and would enjoy each other's company. For one thing, they both share eccentric behavior. Jolie has her odd interest in knives and blood. Thornton admits to having strange phobias. He fears Komodo dragons, certain types of cutlery, and some antique furniture, which he says can be full of dust and make people sick.[1] He is almost always seen in public wearing some kind of hat, usually a baseball cap.

After both were signed to make *Pushing Tin,* they traveled to Toronto, Ontario, to film the movie. One day they accidentally got into the same elevator. Thornton introduced himself to Jolie. He simply said, "I'm Billy Bob—how are you doing?"[2]

Thornton recalled that he was awestruck by Jolie. He said, "And then we came out of the elevator, and I just remember . . . you know wanting something to not go away? Wishing the elevator had gone to China. It's like a bolt of lightning. Something different that never happened before."[3]

As he got into a van, he told Jolie he was going clothes shopping. He asked her if she wanted to come along. Without thinking, Jolie quickly said, "No." After the van drove away, Jolie went around a corner and sat down against a wall. She remembered, "I was just confused. I became a complete idiot."[4]

They did have dinner together with two other people one evening in Toronto. Yet even though they found each other attractive, Thornton was engaged to another actress, Laura Dern.

Pushing Tin was released on April 23, 1999. It received mixed reviews. The majority seemed to say *Pushing Tin* was a good movie that could have been better. Respected critic Leonard Maltin wrote that the movie starts off "extremely well, with strong performances and snappy repartee, but crash-lands in its second half, becoming a dull, domestic romantic comedy."[5]

Thornton and Jolie did not talk for several months after making *Pushing Tin.* Then they started having phone conversations. She thought about him constantly and even got tattoos of his name on her body. Soon, they were seeing each other regularly. Thornton ended his relationship with Laura Dern. Some gossip columnists blamed Jolie for causing Thornton and Dern to break up.

Meanwhile, Jolie's movies continued to find their way into theaters. In the crime drama *The Bone Collector,* she plays a troubled police officer trying to track down a murderer. Most critics did not like it, but it did draw many moviegoers. Between theaters in both the United States and overseas, it earned more than twice as much money as it cost to make.[6]

Late in 1999, the movie *Girl, Interrupted* was released. It tells the story of one girl's year in an institution for the mentally ill in the late 1960s. Jolie plays Lisa, a loud,

Billy Bob Thornton and Angelina Jolie perform together in a scene from *Pushing Tin*.

brash, and rebellious patient. To prepare for the part, Jolie spent three months in a real institution.[7]

In *Girl, Interrupted* Jolie plays a supporting role. The lead role is played by Winona Ryder. Many thought the movie could be a breakout role for Ryder—a role that could make her a superstar. However, once they saw the movie, the critics had mixed feelings. Some said *Girl, Interrupted* carefully avoided clichés while others said it was filled with clichés. Critic Kenneth Turan of the *Los Angeles Times* said that while we know the girls in the movie are "only acting," they make the movie seem very "believable."[8] On the other hand, Peter Stack of the *San Francisco Chronicle* called the movie "light, sappy and mostly unsatisfying."[9]

But critic Jack Garner of the *Rochester Democrat and Chronicle* was right on target. He wrote, "Lisa is played with electrifying energy by Angelina Jolie in a performance guaranteed to secure an Oscar nomination."[10]

Jolie won another Golden Globe for her performance. As Garner predicted, she was nominated for an Oscar for best supporting actress. That was a personal compliment for Jolie, since it was the only major Oscar nomination the movie received. Jolie was not only nominated but she won the big one—the Oscar Award for her dynamic portrayal of Lisa!

Girl, Interrupted producer Douglas Wick compared Jolie to legendary actor Jack Nicholson, who had won an Oscar for best actor many years earlier for his lead role in *One Flew Over the Cuckoo's Nest.* That was another movie about life in a mental institution. Wick said, "Lisa does terrible things. The amazing thing about Angelina is that she has something that Jack Nicholson has which is that she can do very bad things and somehow do them in a way that she remains fascinating."[11]

In April 2000, Jolie and Jonny Lee Miller officially divorced. Then, on May 5, Jolie and Thornton were married in a Las Vegas wedding chapel. These chapels cater mostly to couples who want quick and informal weddings. Jolie wore a blue sleeveless sweater and jeans. Thornton wore jeans and a baseball cap. Some reporters said Jolie wore a vial of Thornton's blood around her neck. Jolie scoffed at those claims. She said it was only a fingerprint.[12]

The wedding ceremony was a surprise to nearly everyone who knew the couple. When Thornton reserved the chapel, he gave his name as Bill Thornton. Chapel owner Greg Smith said, "I didn't know it was him until they got here."[13]

Jolie's father did not attend. Her brother, whom she is so close to, did not attend either. The wedding was a very low-key event.

Winona Ryder and Angelina Jolie in a scene from *Girl, Interrupted*. The film proved to be a breakthrough performance for Jolie.

Although she was getting married for the second time, it was Thornton's fifth marriage. There is a big age difference between Jolie and Thornton. She was twenty-four years old; he was forty-four. Since many critics feel she is much better-looking than Thornton, some described the couple as beauty and the beast, after the famous fairy tale. Jolie did not care. She had stated that she did not take marriage lightly, saying, "I view marriage . . . as an amazing, wonderful thing."[14]

Shortly after her wedding, Jolie's next movie, *Gone in 60 Seconds,* was released. It is an action drama about a car theft ring. Jolie had a small part, which may have been a plus since the movie received mostly terrible reviews. *Variety* said it was "perfectly dreadful in every respect."[15] However, one critic gave Jolie a back-handed compliment. Eugene Novikov of the Web site *filmblather.com* trashed the movie but added, "Maybe more Angelina Jolie would have helped."[16] Regardless of the horrible reviews, *Gone in 60 Seconds* cost only $90 million to make and earned back over $237 million worldwide.[17]

After her critical acclaim in her movies of the late 1990s, Jolie seemed stuck in a rut. Her next movie, *Lara Croft: Tomb Raider,* was based on the Tomb Raider videogame. Like *Gone in 60 Seconds,* it was disliked by most critics. That was not surprising since many critics believe video games do not translate well into movies. Yet, as with *Gone in 60 Seconds,* people went to see *Lara Croft* in droves. The movie was made for $115 million and earned more than $274 million worldwide.[18]

In *Lara Croft,* Jolie was the star. Her job was as tough as her roles in *Gia, George Wallace,* and *Girl, Interrupted.* While Jolie had to speak with a convincing southern accent in *George Wallace,* in *Lara Croft: Tomb Raider* she had to speak in a realistic British accent.

Jolie accepts her Oscar during the 72nd Academy
Awards ceremony on March 26, 2000.

The British accent was not Jolie's only challenge. She also had to learn kickboxing, yoga, weapons training, sled-dog racing, and motorbike racing. Jolie said on the movie set, "When I first got here I felt like this little geek, this scrawny, young actress from LA. I was extremely out of shape. I had not gone to the gym in years. And then through all the training, my body had changed and my mind had changed because I had a totally different focus."[19]

The movie's director, Simon West, stated, "I knew I was going to have to put Angie through some pretty rigorous training. I brought her to London and basically put her into boot camp because there were so many different disciplines that she was going to have to learn."[20] West added, "Angie worked six days a week doing six or seven disciplines per day to get her into shape for the film [including] special weight training. . . . [And] she had to go on special diets."[21]

West expected to use stunt doubles, but Jolie did her own stunts. These included doing double and triple somersaults attached to a bungee chord. The final result had Jolie playing a convincing crime fighter.

Critic Jack Garner of the *Rochester Democrat and Chronicle* wrote, "Jolie also handles the role's considerable physical demands with aplomb. Whether she's bouncing from the ceiling on bungee chords or diving off a dam or coming at you with two guns blazing or zooming by on a motorcycle, she makes us believe she does it every day. She's so absolutely right for the role— it's impossible to conceive anyone else doing it."[22]

Jolie also shared a special moment with her father during the filming. She suggested that Jon Voight play Lord Richard Croft, Lara's father. Voight said, "It was very wonderful to know she wanted to work with me and we had a wonderful time."[23]

Sleeping With the Spiders

It was about this time that Jolie took her UNHCR goodwill trip to Sierra Leona and Tanzania. She left the United States on February 20, 2001, and arrived in Sierra Leone the next day. For a couple of days she met with UNHCR personnel and other officials. Finally, she was assigned a security guard and allowed to enter refugee camps. She was amazed at the positive attitudes of children, despite their situations.

Jolie wrote, "The children here grab your hands and walk with you, smiling and singing. They have nothing. They are wearing ripped dusty clothes and they are smiling. . . . They are so happy to have what little they have now. They are no longer alone or in fear for their safety. Most of them had to walk many, many miles for days with no food or water."[1]

The children found her tattoos funny. They asked her, "Who stamped you?"[2] At another camp, she tried to give out food to the refugees. There were not enough plates to go around so the award-winning Hollywood star washed dirty plates alongside the other volunteers.

Jolie flew home on March 9. But on July 16 she left for another trip—this time to Cambodia. While she was on board the airplane to Cambodia, she wrote in a journal, "Maybe I think I should feel guilty for my ability to come and go from these places when others have no choice. I know one thing. I know I appreciate everything more. I am so grateful for my life."[3]

While in Cambodia she connected with a group called Hazardous Areas Life-Support Organization (HALO). HALO is not a government organization. It consists of people who want to remove the remaining hazards of war. Through HALO, Jolie met people who had lost body parts after accidentally stepping on land mines.

At one point HALO staff members allowed Jolie to detonate a land mine. She said, "It was a great feeling because you know something like that, if HALO hadn't been there and if you weren't detonating it, that it might otherwise be hurting someone, and you are getting rid of something that could be otherwise dangerous or deadly. So it is a great feeling."[4]

Despite her movie star status, Jolie stayed in the same barracks-type lodging as the other HALO workers. Even though she had mosquito netting around her bed, she still was stung by spiders that managed to crawl through. Her feet swelled and constantly itched. She did not eat very much during the day or sleep well at night. She had a constant fear that she might accidentally step on a land mine. Since there were no bathrooms in the barracks, she had to use bushes outdoors. In the black of night there was no telling when she might wander off a marked safe path into a landmine area.

Jolie said, "It's crazy the thought that you really don't know, and for people to live like that all the time."[5] But she also said, "And yet with all of these complaints I have never felt so good in my life. I am tremendously honored to be with these people. I realize more every day how fortunate I have been in my life. I hope I never forget and never complain again about anything."[6]

In her little spare time Jolie continued to work at her craft. Her next movie, *Original Sin,* was released on August 3. It was about a strange romance between an American played by Jolie and a Cuban played by Antonio Banderas. The critics almost unanimously trashed it.

The general complaints were that the direction was poor, the dialogue seemed phony, and the plot was predictable. The movie did not do well with ticket buyers either. It cost about $42 million to make and even with foreign and American audiences combined it made back a meager $35 million.[7]

Some celebrities who give their time or money to charities are believed to do so mainly for publicity. But by now the UNHCR realized that Jolie was very sincere in her humanitarian work. So in August 2001 the UNHCR named her a goodwill ambassador. As a goodwill ambassador, she was given an official go-ahead to keep doing what she had been doing—helping refugees by distributing food and other necessary supplies and gathering information.

UNHCR spokeswoman Tina Ghelli said, "Thanks to Angelina's involvement, UNHCR is now getting tons of inquiries from young people wanting to help the cause. She has also donated more than a million dollars, and she insists on paying for all her own expenses on all of her trips."[8]

From August 17 through August 26, 2001, Jolie went on a mission to Pakistan. In 2001, the neighboring nation of Afghanistan was ruled by a militant regime called the Taliban. These Muslim extremists ruled with a very strict interpretation of the Muslim holy book, the Koran. In doing so the Taliban outlawed everything from flying kites to listening to music from the United States and Europe. The Taliban also made it mandatory for all citizens of Afghanistan to pray at all specified Muslim prayer times.

Under the Taliban, women were subject to especially tough laws. They were forced to wear burqas, or hooded dresses that cover the entire body with just holes for eyes. Women were not allowed to work, drive, or be seen alone in public.

Both men and women who disobeyed the Taliban's laws were often beaten or killed. Some escaped to the neighboring nation, Pakistan. There they lived the miserable lives of refugees.

Pakistan is also a conservative Muslim nation. Its leaders are not as extreme as the Taliban, but they also enforce strict laws based on the Koran. When she arrived in Pakistan, Jolie was told there were certain rules she had to obey. She was not allowed to shake hands with or even make eye contact with a man. She always had to cover her head in public. For her safety she had an armed guard wherever she went.

In her travels through Pakistan, Jolie visited a women's shelter made of sheets stretched over sticks. Another time she went to an urban slum where both adults and children lived off food that had been thrown away. On yet another trip she went to a refugee medical center run by the UNHCR. The patients were treated in small rooms with old tables and dusty carpets. Several patients suffered from polio, an illness that affects the spinal cord and muscles. Most other patients had bullet wounds, burns, and landmine injuries. Over half the patients were children under five.[9]

Jolie wrote, "Some people complain and say UNHCR should do more to help the refugees. This is hard for the staff to hear. These people simply don't understand the limited funds and cutbacks."[10]

On September 11, 2001, terrorist attacks took place in the United States. This was roughly two weeks after Jolie had returned home from Pakistan. Almost three thousand people were killed in the attacks that day. The vast majority of victims were inside the twin towers of the World Trade Center in New York City.

The terrorists were part of a group called Al Qaeda. Al Qaeda is led by a Saudi Arabian man named Osama bin Laden, who had been living in Taliban-controlled Afghanistan. Many Americans were looking for scapegoats beyond the actual Al Qaeda terrorists. Some wanted to blame all Afghans.

Jolie's trip to Pakistan and the poverty she witnessed were fresh in her mind. Shortly after the September 11 attacks, Jolie publicly spoke out about the Afghan

Angelina Jolie with her son, Maddox, in 2007.
Jolie adopted Maddox in 2001.

refugees' need for help. She also gave a donation to help the Afghan refugees in Pakistan. In response she received three death threats. One man found her private telephone number and called her. He said he wished for everyone in her family to die. Jolie took it in stride. She merely responded, "Emotions were running high, I understand that. It was a difficult time for everyone."[11]

In the fall Jolie and Thornton took the first step on a life-changing path. They decided to adopt a child from one of the refugee camps Jolie visited. Since Jolie had a special place in her heart for the people of Cambodia, she adopted a Cambodian child. This would be Thornton's first UNHCR-related trip. In November 2001 the two went to a Cambodian orphanage, where about fifteen children lived. Jolie fell in love with a three-month-old boy whom she adopted and named Maddox.

Jolie recalled, "Maddox was the last child I saw. And he was asleep, and they put him in my arms and he stayed asleep. And then he opened his eyes and he smiled. He stared at me for two minutes and then he smiled. And I cried. And I felt this kid is okay being in my arms, and accepts me."[12]

"Don't Go Off the Path"

Jolie could not take the little boy home right away. Government agencies have to approve such adoptions. Maddox had to be tested to make sure he did not carry serious diseases. Jolie's and Thornton's backgrounds had to be researched to be certain they would be good parents.

While Jolie was waiting for the adoption to go through, her next movie was released. It was a comedy-fantasy titled *Life or Something Like It*. It premiered in theaters on April 26, 2002. Jolie's role was as a hard-working television reporter who learns she has only one week to live. She then decides to literally live as if it is her last week on earth. *Life or Something Like It* fared better than *Original Sin* but was no blockbuster. Still, most critics liked it. Mick LaSalle of the *San Francisco Chronicle* wrote, "The result is a worthy woman's film and Jolie's best showcase to date."[1]

On May 8, 2002, Maddox was permanently united with Jolie and Thornton. At the time, she was in Africa filming the movie *Beyond Borders*. It was a romantic drama about two people who fall in love as they work with refugees in poor countries. It was a subject Jolie could certainly identify with. Meanwhile, Thornton was not spending much time with Jolie or their new child. He was busy playing with a blues band he had started called the Boxmasters.

Jolie spent most of 2002 as one of the airline industry's best customers. She went on more UNHCR field missions to other troubled lands, including Namibia, Thailand, Kenya, and Ecuador. As she traveled, she and Thornton saw less and less of each other. Her trip to Ecuador, which took place in June, was her first time away from Maddox. She left her son with her mother and brother. She wrote, "It was ridiculous how emotional I felt kissing him goodbye."[2]

Jolie did her usual hard work in Ecuador. About seven thousand refugees from the neighboring nation of Colombia were living there.[3] Colombia was the site of rampant guerilla warfare. Some of it was due to rivalries between professional drug gangs. She said about her experience in Ecuador, "What was really shocking was that every individual person you meet will tell you that their immediate family was [affected]. . . . Somebody's child was killed, somebody's husband. Someone was beaten."[4]

By July, Jolie and Thornton decided to divorce. It would take some months until the divorce became official. Meanwhile, Jolie's relationship with her father took a bizarre turn. Voight hand-delivered Jolie a letter saying he did not like her traveling to dangerous places. But that was just the start of his message. Jolie said that her father "said some very ugly things to me about what he thought I was like as a person and how I was conducting my life."[5] She showed the letter to her mother and brother. They were just as upset as Jolie was.[6]

Jolie ignored the letter, and avoided any contact with her father. Then, on August 2, 2002, Voight appeared on the entertainment news television program *Access Hollywood*. Voight was teary-eyed and confessed he was "brokenhearted . . . because I've been trying to reach my daughter and get her help, and I have failed and I'm sorry. Really I haven't come forward and addressed the serious mental problems she has spoken about so candidly to the press over the years, but I've tried behind the scenes in every way."[7]

He added that she began showing signs of mental illness as a baby.[8] Voight said that he wanted to be a good grandfather. He admitted that he had never seen his grandchild, Maddox. He confessed, "That is the greatest pain."[9]

On the one hand, Voight blamed himself for his problems with Jolie. He seemed like he wanted to make amends with her. At the time, Jolie was getting ready to shoot the sequel to *Lara Croft: Tomb Raider.* She was upset that he aired their personal problems on national television.[10] The fact that he questioned her mental health disturbed her the most.[11]

In response, Jolie did not speak to reporters directly. However, she did release a statement. It read: "'I don't want to make public the reasons for my bad relationship with my father. I will only say that, like every child, [brother] Jamie and I would have loved to have had a warm and loving relationship with our dad. After all these years, I have determined that it is not healthy for me to be around my father, especially now that I am responsible for my own child."[12]

The producer of the *Lara Croft* sequel, Lawrence Gordon, publicly defended Jolie. He said there was

Jolie speaks at a news conference in Quito, Ecuador, on June 10, 2002.

nothing wrong with her mentally. Gordon stated, "If there was a problem, I would know it."[13]

Despite her personal issues, Jolie still had her acting career and her humanitarian work. During Christmas week of 2002, she traveled to Kosovo in southeastern Europe, a region of Serbia that was struggling for independence. She left Maddox with a nanny. She wrote, "I'm sure when he is older he will understand."[14]

As she talked to the refugees, she heard horrible stories of war between people from Kosovo and Serbia. These included living through car bomb attacks and landmine explosions. She described the conditions: "The air is so clear it is very cold. You realized it after a while, and wonder how they live in it. There is no real source of heat. Most windows are broken and many of the houses have no roofs."[15]

Shortly afterward, she said, "I would never complain again about the stupid things I used to complain about, or be self destructive, or not realize on a daily basis how lucky I am to have a roof over my head and enough food to eat and that my son is healthy."[16]

Jolie kept up her hectic pace in 2003. In the early spring she embarked on another trip for the UNHCR. This time it was to the island nation of Sri Lanka, just south of India in the Indian Ocean. Sri Lanka has been a victim of ongoing civil war since the 1980s. As a result, the nation is pockmarked with land mines and other unexploded weapons. Many residents live in shabby shelters with shortages of food, water, and sanitation facilities.

Jolie described one house in which a family of three generations returned after being displaced for seven years. She wrote, "I look at the house and there is no roof, a broken water well, and big holes from bombs and shells in all walls. This small building houses eight people living in three rooms."[17]

On another occasion in Sri Lanka, Jolie was taken to a home for orphaned and abandoned girls. There were more than five hundred children there between the ages of one and sixteen. It was here that the threat of land mines truly touched Jolie. She wrote, "We walk to visit the babies and toddlers. 'Don't go off the path,' I am told. 'It's not de-mined yet.' My God, just a few feet away from all these children, there are land mines. It makes me so angry."[18]

Meanwhile, her divorce from Thornton became official on May 27, 2003. And she could not escape questions about her relationship with her father. She finally realized she could not run away from the topic. She answered reporters' questions but never resorted to calling her father a bad person.

In one 2003 interview, she spoke with a reporter from the British Broadcasting Corporation (BBC) program *Radio Times.* She conceded that she no longer had respect for her father's opinions. She explained, "I no longer see us as father and daughter. . . . I won't have unhealthy relationships in my life. That's why it was easy for me to divorce, and easy for me not to speak to my father. I don't regret it."[19]

The long-awaited sequel to *Lara Croft: Tomb Raider* was released on July 25, 2003. It was titled *Lara Croft Tomb Raider: The Cradle of Life.* Like Jolie's first *Lara Croft* movie, the reviews were mostly negative. In fact, one critic, Daniel M. Kimmel of the *Worcester* (Mass.) *Telegram and Gazette,* wrote, "The new 'Lara Croft' has no reason to exist except that the first one made money."[20] On one account Kimmel was right. Lara Croft video game fans loved the movie, and it did make a lot of money. The cost to make it was $95 million. It earned back more than $156 million worldwide.[21]

Jolie's next destination for the UNHCR was Russia, which was involved in a civil war with its republic of Chechnya. The Muslim majority in Chechnya had declared its independence.[22] Russia was fighting to keep Chechnya from breaking away.

On August 19, a few days before Jolie was about to leave the United States, a terrorist driving a car bomb attacked the United Nations headquarters in Baghdad, Iraq. A total of twenty-two UN staff members were killed and more than one hundred were injured.[23] The next day UN officials called Jolie to ask her if she would prefer to cancel her trip to Russia. They said her schedule had been leaked to the public in Russia. Jolie responded, "No. There has always been a security concern."[24]

Before going to Chechnya, Jolie arrived in Moscow, the Russian capital, on August 21. That night she had an official dinner with Russian diplomats. Jolie said the building where they dined looked more like a museum than a home to government offices. She admitted feeling uneasy. She did not know if she was allowed to sit on the exquisite furniture. She listened to the Russians explain their side of the Chechnya situation. They stressed that Chechnya is a part of Russia and not a separate country.

Although many of the world's citizens felt Russia was wrong, Jolie did not play politics. She wrote that the diplomats "seem like such good men."[25] She added, "They speak of the needs of the Chechen people, how the government has been working with some Chechen NGO's [non-governmental organizations] and civilians in the last two years successfully and about money being set aside for people to rebuild their homes. They say shelter is the first priority, of course, then security.

I know UNHCR feels security is first. But I realize it is complicated."[26]

On the airplane on her way home from Chechnya, she wrote, "Sitting on [the] plane once again returning to the safety of my home, my country and my son. I always feel guilty leaving because it is so easy for me."[27] On October 24, Jolie's movie *Beyond Borders* was released. Unfortunately, it was poorly reviewed. Unlike the Lara Croft movies, *Beyond Borders* lost money. It cost $35 million to make but earned only $11.7 million worldwide.[28] One critic, James Berardinelli of *ReelViews.com* wrote, "The film's heart is undoubtedly in the right place, but so what? . . . For a film like *Beyond Borders* to work, we have to care about the characters and their situations."[29] Berardinelli said that the script was too weak for audiences to care about the characters.

Around this time, Jolie published a book based on her journals from her first four trips for the UNHCR. It was simply titled, *Notes from My Travels.* In the book's foreword, United Nations High Commissioner for Refugees Ruud Lubbers wrote, "Since her appointment as a Goodwill Ambassador, Angelina has more than fulfilled my expectations. She has proven to be a close partner and a genuine colleague in our efforts to find solutions for the world's refugees. Above all, she has

Nane Annan, wife of UN Secretary General Kofi Annan, presents Angelina Jolie with the United Nations Correspondents Association Citizen of the World Award on October 22, 2003.

helped to make the tragedy of refugees real to everyone who will listen."[30]

Her book is still selling today, several years after she wrote it.

On October 23, Jolie was again honored by the UN. She received the first Citizen of the World Award from the UN Correspondents' Association. As she held back tears, Jolie said she was "inspired and humbled" to work with the world's refugees.[31]

Darfur and the Janjaweed

Although Jolie always seemed to be on the go to some place where refugees were suffering, she did more than donate her time, caring, and energy. She also donated millions of dollars. She gave fifty thousand British pounds, or about seventy-two thousand U.S. dollars, to a children's hospital in Liverpool, England, after its staff treated Maddox while she was making a film nearby.[1,2] Maddox had suffered minor injuries after an accident with a hot teakettle. The money was slated to help build a new cancer unit at the hospital.

On another occasion she donated five hundred thousand dollars to the UNHCR's new National Center for Refugee and Immigrant Children.[3] By 2003 she had donated a total of more than $3 million to the UNHCR.[4] Jolie has also been very generous to the people of Cambodia. She spent five million dollars to build a wildlife refuge in poverty-stricken northwestern Cambodia.[5] Nearby she built a home for herself and her family. It is in Cambodian style, and consists of little more than three huts on stilts. Inside are hammocks for sleeping and only the most basic plumbing. She feels it is good for Maddox to spend time in such a place to better get to know and understand his culture.[6]

The same year she also created the Maddox Jolie Project (MJP). It is an organization based in Cambodia's poor northwestern region. Its first goals are to preserve the nation's forests, endangered species, and freshwater ecosystems.

In December, Jolie's destination was the Middle Eastern kingdom of Jordan. There she worked with refugees escaping the Iraq War. Since the refugee camp is so close to the Iraqi border, Jolie was forced to travel in a military helicopter. At that time, about five hundred people lived in the camp. About one hundred were under age eighteen. Most were Palestinians who had been rejected by the Iraqis because they were not ethnic Iraqis. They were forced to leave Iraq when the war started. Others were from countries such as Sudan and Somalia.

The conditions were harsh—colder at night than in Iraq, and with only basic necessities. One girl refugee, about eight years old said, "We were living in Baghdad [the capital of Iraq] in peace. Then the first day of war we were very frightened from all the bombs and missiles."[7] A woman refugee added, "We were humiliated in Iraq as Palestinians. But at least for that while, we felt safe, then that changed. Here we feel safe from war but we know we cannot live here forever and don't know where else we can go."[8]

At one point, Jolie met with Jordan's Queen Noor. Jolie found that she and the American-born queen shared a common approach to the Middle East. Jolie said of the queen, "You ask her opinion, and she doesn't have any anger. She seems to be coming from a really balanced place of love."[9]

In April 2004, Jolie made her first humanitarian visit within the United States. Her destinations were three camps in Arizona for people seeking asylum, or a place to live in safety, in the United States. Every year, thousands escape bad situations in their home countries and seek safe lives in the United States. More than six thousand refugees who came to the United States in 2004 were children.[10]

Many of these refugee children came without adults. Some were child soldiers or victims of sexual abuse.

Angelina Jolie listens to a wheelchair-bound woman during one of her visits to Iraq. The woman was one of 1,300 refugees stuck in the Al Waleed refugee camp in Iraq, unable to leave for Syria.

Others were homeless, while some were forced into marriage despite the fact they are children. Yet others were exploited by Americans who abducted them. They forced them to work as child laborers in factories or as prostitutes.

A U.S. government department called the Office of Refugee Resettlement (ORR) was at first responsible for the well-being of these children. In 2003, the UNHCR was allowed to share responsibility for the children with the ORR. Jolie was most moved by children who were on their own. She said, "Many of these children have survived tragedy, so being separated from their families can only add to their suffering."[11]

Unlike the shacks surrounded by land mines where children lived in impoverished nations, by comparison these children in the United States lived in comfort. Their homes were dormitories. They were kept busy with craft projects and workshops to learn skills. As she was about to leave Arizona, Jolie admitted, "I am excited that the UNHCR is working with ORR on this initiative. . . . These children are survivors. I am awed by their spirit and inspired by their resilience."[12]

Between being an actor, a humanitarian, and a mother, it would seem that Jolie did not have enough time to sleep. Yet she still found time to act in five movies released in 2004. And in addition to her Arizona trip, Jolie made research trips to Africa and Asia. But probably the most noteworthy journey she took was to a troubled land in Africa called Darfur.

Darfur is a district in the western part of the African nation of Sudan. Some residents of Darfur, mainly black Africans, are victims of genocide at the hands of the government of Sudan. The Sudanese militia, known as the Janjaweed, are mainly of Arabic descent. The Janjaweed were conducting raids against the civilians of Darfur. They uprooted Darfur residents from their homes. The Janjaweed also committed violent crimes against the people of Darfur, including rape and murder. The situation in Darfur had caught the attention of the world. Yet no one seemed to be able to do anything about ending the genocide.

The UNHCR estimated in 2004 that there were about 1.6 million displaced persons from Darfur.[13] Some one hundred fifty-eight thousand were able to escape to eleven refugee camps in the neighboring country of Chad.[14] In June, Jolie went to Chad and heard horrific tales from the refugees from Darfur. In one case, a woman told Jolie how the Janjaweed militia raided her village, shooting at civilians, ransacking buildings, and burning people's homes.

As well as talking with refugees, Jolie does not mind getting her hands dirty. She helped newly arrived Darfur refugees load their meager possessions onto trucks to be taken to refugee camps. She served food to refugees, and helped weigh and measure refugee children as part of medical examinations to check for malnourishment.

In October Jolie went to the region again. This time she went into Darfur itself. She heard about children who were sexually abused by Janjaweed militiamen. She met children who had no access to schools or medical care.

Jolie then held a press conference. She told reporters that the UNHCR needed much more money to protect and aid displaced persons from Darfur. That was despite the fact that the UNHCR had already spent $115 million on helping Darfur refugees over the last three months.[15] Another big problem was physical access to the refugees. The government of Sudan was doing all it could to block access to those who wished to help.

Jolie's last goodwill trips in 2004 were to Thailand and Lebanon. Being paid for acting helped fund her travels. Jolie explained, "I'm able to take the money and see a hospital built or build a well somewhere. So now when I return [to Hollywood] I'm half working for my family and my son, and half working to send it back into places. It makes me all that more eager to go to work and be successful because I know I can do good things."[16]

The movies she appeared in during 2004 ranged from *Alexander,* a nearly-three-hour-long historical epic about Alexander the Great, to *Shark Tale,* a feature cartoon about a gangster shark. The cartoon received better reviews than *Alexander.* In *Shark Tale,* Jolie is the voice of a glamorous fish named Lola who tries to steal the fish hero, voiced by Will Smith, from his girlfriend. Jolie said voicing a cartoon character was a pleasure.

"One, it's just fun to go to work in your pajamas with no makeup on. . . . But it's funny to see yourself as

Oscar and Lola (voiced by Will Smith and Angelina Jolie, respectively), two of the animated fish characters in *Shark Tale*.

a fish." Jolie laughed, "They showed me the pictures of all the different fish, and I saw my fish, and it was so apparent to me very quickly that that was my fish. . . . I have a kid now, so he can watch *Shark Tale*. Even though Mommy is the bad fish, I think he'll like Mommy's fish."[17]

Jolie's mother questioned why Angie was cast to play the troublemaker. She asked her daughter, "Why would they cast you as the bad fish? Why didn't they make you the angelfish? Your name is Angie." Jolie replied, "Because, Mom, the world doesn't see me as you see me."[18]

During the filming of *Alexander*, Jolie's name was once again all over the gossip pages. Rumors spread that she was dating her costar, Colin Farrell. He was known as a wild man just as much as Jolie was regarded as a wild woman. Interestingly, in the movie Farrell played Alexander while Jolie played his mother, Olympias. In real life, Farrell is just one year younger than Jolie. Another rumor was that Jolie was dating Val Kilmer, the man who played her husband, King Philip II of Macedonia. Even though many who know the three actors said there was no romance between any of them, the rumors persisted.

> "Mom, the world doesn't see me as you see me."

Jolie's character spent much of the film covered in snakes. In fact, when she was not part of a scene, Jolie spent much of her spare time with the snakes. Since she had kept snakes as pets as a child, she enjoyed getting to know them better.

Before *Alexander* was released, both movie critics and fans expected it to be a blockbuster. But just the opposite happened. Nearly every critic hated it. Some said the script was boring. Others complained that the director, Oliver Stone, took too many liberties with the historical truth. One common gripe was that Colin Farrell was miscast as Alexander. Farrell was born in Ireland and was unable to hide his Irish accent.

Jolie was not spared criticism either. Even though she mastered a southern accent in *George Wallace* and a British accent in the *Lara Croft* movies, she was blasted for an unconvincing accent in *Alexander*. Critic Rick Groen of the *Toronto Globe and Mail* called her accent an "Eastern European mishmash."[19] In short, *Alexander* was a complete disaster. It cost $155 million to make but earned back only $34 million domestically.[20]

Jolie's three other movies in 2004 were wildly different from one another. They were also little-seen except by Jolie fans. In *Taking Lives,* Jolie played an FBI agent trying to solve a murder mystery. She had a small role in a movie about world politics titled *The Fever.* Her "fun" role that year was costarring in *Sky Captain and the World of Tomorrow.* It is a throwback to the good versus evil science-fiction melodramas from the 1930s. Even though the movie features giant robots and airplane pilots, all the filming was done in front of a blue screen. The action scenes were all computer-generated.

The majority of critics liked *Sky Captain. Boston Globe* reviewer Ty Burr wrote that the movie is "a glorious labor of love."[21] Burr added that Jolie "is a joy as Capt. Frankie Cook, eye-patched British commanding officer of a floating air force base that takes the travelers in. Barking out lines like, 'Alert the amphibious squadron!,' Jolie finds the pulse of the movie and rides it for the few scenes she's in."[22]

During 2004 Jolie was also filming a major role in a movie scheduled to come out in 2005. She would have a major role in it. Like previous movies, *Mr. and Mrs. Smith* would play a big part in her real life.

Mr. and Mrs. Smith Fall in Love

In *Mr. and Mrs. Smith,* Jolie plays Jane Smith, who is married to John Smith, played by Brad Pitt. On the surface they seem to be an average couple. But neither Jane nor John realizes that both are professional hired killers. They then learn that each is hired to kill the other one. The movie has plenty of action and drama, and most critics enjoyed it.

But there was drama behind the scenes, too. When the actors began making the movie, Pitt was married to Jennifer Aniston, an actress best known for playing Rachel on the long-running television comedy *Friends.* Pitt is known as one of the movie industry's handsomest actors and Aniston is regarded as one of the business's prettiest. They were viewed by many entertainment writers and fans as Hollywood's sweethearts.

During the months Jolie and Pitt spent making *Mr. and Mrs. Smith,* people noticed that the two were spending a lot of time with each other. That made sense to a degree since they were lead actors in the same movie. But they seemed to be together even when they were not filming scenes.

Entertainment reporters asked Pitt and Jolie if there were romantic feelings between them. Jolie told reporters that she and Pitt were just friends. Pitt said that he was happily married to Aniston. Yet Pitt and Jolie were sharing a secret they could not keep private for long. Photographs of the two together appeared in gossip publications. Some people on the film set had no problem telling reporters the truth: Jolie and Pitt had fallen in love.

One person who knew both Pitt and Jolie confessed that Pitt was won over not only by Jolie's beauty and charm. She said that Pitt found Jolie's charity work very attractive.[1] Before long, the news that Jolie and Pitt were a couple was out in the open.

While much of the public admires Jolie for her heart of gold in helping the world's neediest people, they look down on her personal life. They blame her for stealing other women's husbands or boyfriends.[2] Back when her mother had asked her why she played the bad fish instead of the angel fish in *Shark Tale,* Jolie answered that was how people saw her. This was a perfect example.

In May 2005, Jolie took another goodwill trip to Pakistan. Despite all the poverty around her, she noticed some good things. She witnessed a convoy of trucks carrying five hundred refugees living in Pakistan back to their native Afghanistan.[3] That was just a tiny portion of the more than fifty-five thousand refugees who had returned to Afghanistan since March that year.[4]

Rumors then started circulating in the media that Jolie was expecting a child. The rumors were technically true, but not in the way most people imagined. In early July, she and Pitt flew to Ethiopia, a very poor nation in Africa. On July 6, Jolie officially adopted another child, an Ethiopian infant girl who was orphaned after her mother died of AIDS. Although Pitt was with her during the adoption, Jolie stressed that the decision to adopt another child was hers alone. She said she always wanted a family of more than three.[5]

Why did she choose an Ethiopian child? One journalist said Jolie "has a hunger about the world and helping people. The whole world is important to Angie, but she's very attached to Africa as a continent. Africa is a country of survivors. She identifies."[6] Jolie named the

Brad Pitt and Angelina Jolie in a scene from *Mr. And Mrs. Smith* (2005).

infant girl Zahara Marley Jolie. "Zahara" means "flower" in Hebrew. Marley came from the Jamaican reggae music legend Bob Marley. Yet not soon after Jolie brought Zahara to back New York City, she noticed something was wrong with the baby. Zahara was seriously underweight, had no interest in drinking milk, and had a fungus infection in her mouth. Jolie was afraid that the baby would not live.[7] Julie Aronson, a doctor who specializes in babies adopted from other countries, examined Zahara. She discovered Zahara was suffering from malnutrition and dehydration. But what was causing it? Zahara was sent to the emergency room at a New York City hospital. After much testing, Dr. Aronson learned that Zahara had a salmonella infection. Salmonella is a bacteria that attacks the digestive system. Zahara spent six days in the hospital. Dr. Aronson said of Jolie, "She was there 24 hours a day, keeping watch. She kept saying how much she admired her baby. She had so much admiration and respect for Zahara's strength."[8]

Although she visited and helped people in so many nations, Jolie still had special feelings toward the people and places of Cambodia. On July 31, Cambodian King Norodom Sihamoni signed a royal decree making her a citizen of Cambodia. The director of the Cambodian Vision in Development humanitarian organization, Mounh Sarath, declared that Jolie deserved citizenship "not because of the money she has given but [for] her good heart and love" for the Cambodian people.[9] Jolie answered that she was "thrilled" to accept the special honor.[10]

Late that summer, Jolie began filming *The Good Shepherd.* The movie is a spy tale taking place around the time of the founding of the CIA in the 1940s. She took a break from filming on October 11 to accept one of the highest honors any person can receive: the United Nations Global Humanitarian Action Award.

She earned it for all the work she had done over the last several years for the UNHCR.

As she received the honor, Jolie announced to the gathered crowd, "Second to my children, spending time with refugees and other persons of need around the world has been the greatest gift."[11]

The next month Jolie was halfway around the world once more. Again, she was in Pakistan, but not for the usual reason of helping war refugees. A devastating earthquake had struck Pakistan on October 8 and Jolie flew there to do her part. It was reported that seventy-three thousand people had been killed and tens of thousands were homeless.[12] Jolie described the scene, "You fly over the area and you can't believe it. . . . No one sitting at home has any idea what this really looks like. It is un-believable. For 20 minutes flying we saw just one house after another broken. There is nothing standing."[13]

Her partner, Brad Pitt, joined her on this mission. He traveled by helicopter to deliver food to some of the hardest hit and most remote areas.

Then, in December, Pitt made a special commitment to Jolie and to her children. He formally adopted them

> "Second to my children, spending time with refugees and other persons of need around the world has been the greatest gift."

Jolie accepts the 2005 UN Global Humanitarian Action Award from John C. Whitehead on October 11, 2005.

as his children, too. The two also appeared in front of a judge and said they wanted to legally change the children's last name to Jolie-Pitt.

During the filming of *The Good Shepherd* in the Dominican Republican on January 10, 2006, Jolie made a stunning announcement. She and Pitt were expecting a child of their own. Even though she was pregnant, Jolie refused to slow down. That is, until she collapsed during the filming. Doctors told her that the grueling task of making a movie, traveling the world on goodwill missions, and taking care of two young children was too much for a pregnant woman to handle. Thankfully, *The Good Shepherd* was the last movie she had planned to make for a while. Once the filming was finished, she gave herself some much-needed rest.

The couple decided to have their baby in an unusual place: the African nation of Namibia. One reason was that they would be far from the gossip reporters in Los Angeles and New York. Another was because of Jolie's special love and respect for the people of Africa. On the way to Namibia, Brad and Angelina made a stop in Paris. Jolie's mother was living there, and suffering from terminal cancer. For a while, Jolie considered giving birth in Paris to be near her mother, but the couple decided to fulfill their plans to have the baby in Namibia.[14]

Angelina gave birth to a baby girl, Shiloh Nouvel Jolie-Pitt, on May 27. "Shiloh" means "peaceful one" in Hebrew and "Nouvel" means "new" in French. Just two days later, Pitt and Jolie announced they would donate three hundred thousand dollars for maternity ward equipment for two hospitals in Namibia.[15]

Very few friends or relatives were in Namibia to celebrate Shiloh's birth. Jolie's brother James Haven was there. So were Pitt's parents, who flew in from their hometown of Springfield, Missouri. Jolie's mother was too sick to travel. She did send a message, though. It read, "My heart is overflowing with joy with the new arrival of Brad and Angelina's third child. Maddox, Zahara and Shiloh are deeply loved children. They have very kind and caring parents who love and support each other in every way."[16]

> "Maddox, Zahara and Shiloh are deeply loved children."

Since Jolie was estranged from her father, Jon Voight, he was not present. But he did say to a reporter, "I'm so excited; this is wonderful. I am just so very, very happy for both of them. . . . I wish them all the happiness in the world. God bless them both."[17]

Pitt and Jolie returned home two months later to a media circus. Magazines were offering millions of dollars for the first photographs of baby Shiloh. *People* magazine paid $4.1 million for the first rights in North America to run a photo of Shiloh.[18] While some celebrities would be thrilled to have their baby's picture on a magazine cover, Jolie and Pitt truly prefer privacy. They might take their kids to the beach or a local toy store, but they are most comfortable being with each other at home.[19]

To their fans and the media, their privacy did not matter. By this time, Jolie and Pitt were America's favorite glamour couple. The media reported on everything the Jolie-Pitt family did. They even began to refer to the couple by one name: Brangelina. But the two were not inseparable. In the fall of 2006, Pitt was making a movie in the United States while Jolie went to India. The main reason for Jolie's trip was to film a movie about a true-life incident that had horrified much of the world. Shortly after the September 11, 2001, attacks, Islamic terrorists in Pakistan kidnapped Daniel Pearl, an American journalist for the *Wall Street Journal*. The terrorists said Pearl was targeted because he was Jewish and a CIA agent.[20] Pearl was not an agent.[21]

Pearl was killed by the terrorists four weeks later. His captors filmed Pearl's murder by beheading and the footage was available all over the Internet. Pearl's widow, Mariane, wrote a memoir while her husband was held prisoner. It was later titled *A Mighty Heart: The Brave Life and Death of My Husband Daniel Pearl.* Long before he and Jolie were a couple, Pitt had thought the memoir would make a good movie. After Jolie was offered the part of Mariane Pearl, the two met to get to know each other before filming the movie.

The movie production company decided to film in India, a majority Hindu country. They felt it was too dangerous to work in the mostly Muslim nation of Pakistan. Jolie took advantage of her time in India to meet with refugees.

Although India has taken in refugees from several nations, Jolie spent most of her time with those from Afghanistan and the southeast Asian nation of Myanmar (formerly Burma), which is controlled by a dictatorial military government.

> "I came up to Delhi just to visit with you. I am honored to be able to meet you. You are very strong women. You are amazing."

Two Burmese woman told Jolie she looked like an actress. Jolie answered, "That's why I am in India, making a film . . . but I came up to Delhi just to visit with you. I am honored to be able to meet you. You are very strong women. You are amazing."[22] Jolie then met with government officials in India and thanked them for "their longstanding hospitality to refugees."[23]

The next month Pitt joined her as they traveled on a goodwill trip to the Central American nation of Costa Rica. On Christmas Day in Costa Rica, Jolie and Pitt handed out presents to refugees, most from the South American nation of Colombia.

"She's Absolutely Serious"

Jolie was once asked by a reporter if it bothers her that some people think she works with refugees just for publicity—that her goodwill work is more about keeping her name in the headlines than helping others. *Forbes,* a very respected business magazine, wrote that Jolie admitted that she does some charity work to distract the media from negative things she has done.[1]

She has testified before Congress to help get money for the world's refugees. One Senate staff member, Chris Ann Keehner, who worked with Jolie, said, "She [Jolie] fills a room . . . It gives a member of Congress a photo op [opportunity], and it's a way to get the message out—even if she did break up a marriage."[2]

Some comedians have gone so far as to crack jokes about celebrities doing charity work for selfish reasons. Jolie replied, "I don't know, but you think, My God, it actually stops people from doing good things because they're worried that they're going to be made fun of."[3] She added that gossip reporters would jump at the chance to take a photo of an actor such as Jolie working in another nation with a male celebrity, just to imply they are dating.[4]

However, General Colin Powell, a former U.S. secretary of state, said about Jolie, "She's absolutely serious. Her work with refugees is not something to decorate herself. She studies the issues."[5]

At the Golden Globe awards on January 15, 2007, Jolie was dressed as elegantly as one might expect. But observers said she appeared to be very depressed for such a happy occasion. She knew something the reporters did not. Her mother, Marcheline, was in her final battle with cancer. Marcheline died on January 27 at the age of fifty-six. Jolie and her brother, James Haven, said in a press release to *People* magazine, "There are no words to express what an amazing woman and mother she was. She was our best friend."[6] But life went on. More and more of the time, Jolie and Pitt were working together.

In February, Jolie made another goodwill trip to Chad to investigate the situation of refugees from Darfur. While in Chad she wrote an editorial for the *Washington Post,* saying that since her last visit to the area in 2004, more than two hundred thousand people had died and the Janjaweed militia had driven 2.5 million people from their homes.[7] She wrote that she was told to stay in Chad and not go into Darfur because attacks on humanitarian workers were on the rise.

In her editorial, Jolie urged the International Criminal Court (ICC), whose job it is to fight war criminals, to prosecute the Janjaweed and their sponsors. Jolie wrote, "What the worst people in the world fear most is justice. That's what we should deliver."[8] The author description showed how seriously the *Washington Post* takes Jolie's work: "The writer is a goodwill ambassador for the United Nations High Commission for Refugees."[9] There is no mention of her being an actor.

> **"What the worst people in the world fear most is justice. That's what we should deliver."**

Jolie and Pitt made news again but surprised no one when in mid-March they adopted another foreign-born child. This time it was a three-year-old boy from a Vietnamese orphanage. The orphanage director, Nguyen Van

Trung, recalled that, "They [Jolie and her son Maddox] tried to make friends with the Vietnamese boy, who cried when he saw them because for him, they are strangers. . . . Jolie was very moved. Both of them tried to comfort the little boy."[10]

They named their new son Pax Thien Jolie-Pitt. Since Vietnam does not allow unmarried couples to adopt children, Jolie adopted Pax as a single parent and Pitt stayed in New Orleans where he was making the movie *The Curious Case of Benjamin Button.* The name "Pax" is Latin for "peace." "Thien" means "sky" in Vietnamese.

It seems that Jolie spent that entire winter and spring globetrotting. On May 3 she was back in Washington to announce the formation of a group called Global Action for Children (GAC). Its purpose is to increase funding from the United States to educate and support orphans in poor countries. She did not single-handedly form GAC, but she takes an active role. Right away Jolie and Pitt donated $1 million to GAC.[11]

By this time the Maddox Jolie Project had grown like a sunflower. As word of the project spread, more money came in. The MJP became better organized and took on more responsibilities. A statement by the group said their goals were directed toward "eradicating extreme rural poverty, protecting natural resources and conserving wildlife."[12] As Brad Pitt became involved with the MJP, it changed its official name to the Maddox Jolie-Pitt

Foundation. That permitted them to keep the group's acronym, MJP.

The movie *A Mighty Heart* was released on June 22. Jolie received rave reviews for her portrayal of Mariane Pearl. The *Hollywood Reporter* wrote, "Angelina Jolie delivers a well-measured and moving performance."[13] Critic Roger Ebert wrote, "Standing at the center of the story is Mariane Pearl, played by Angelina Jolie in a performance that is both physically and emotionally convincing. . . . Jolie's performance depends above all on inner conviction; she reminds us, as we saw in some of her earlier films like *Girl, Interrupted* (1999), that she is a skilled actress and not merely (however entertainingly) a Tomb Raider."[14]

Despite the strong reviews, at first *A Mighty Heart* did not do well financially. It earned less money in American theaters than it cost to make. However, it made about the same amount in foreign theaters as it did in American ones. In total, it earned back a little more than it cost to produce.[15] Many in the entertainment business were surprised that Jolie was nominated for neither a Golden Globe or an Academy Award.

After *A Mighty Heart,* three more movies featuring Jolie were released in rapid succession. In the epic *Beowulf,* she played the monster Grendel's mother. She then did the voice of Master Tigress in the animated

Jolie listens to an earthquake survivor during her visit to Jabel, Pakistan, on November 26, 2005.

feature *Kung Fu Panda*. Finally, she had a supporting role in the action movie *Wanted*. She played a secret agent who lures a discouraged man to avenge his father's death. *Wanted* took a backseat in publicity to *A Mighty Heart* but still was a hit among critics and audiences.

Jolie also made another trip to the Middle East. She stopped first in Syria to examine the lives of refugees from the Iraq war. The next day she crossed the border into war-ravaged Iraq to visit refugees stuck in a makeshift camp and unable to leave Iraq. Jolie said she was leaving the ideas of political solutions to politicians and was simply there to help war victims. She then separated herself from UNHCR to visit soldiers from the United States and other allied countries.

Tired from her travels and filmmaking, Jolie told a reporter she wanted to take time off to relax. But there was no way someone with her energy and spirit could do nothing. In the fall of 2007, Jolie began filming a murder thriller titled *Changeling*. It is based on an event that took place in Los Angeles in the 1920s. Jolie plays Christine Collins, a woman whose nine-year-old son, Walter, is kidnapped. The Los Angeles police are in a rush to get credit for solving the crime. They return to Christine a boy they claim is Walter. But he is not Walter, and Christine knows he is not her son. In reality, the Los Angeles police force is corrupt. The police try to brainwash Christine into thinking she does not recognize her own son. Throughout the rest of the movie, Christine tries to find out what happened to her real son.

The director of *Changeling* was Academy Award winner Clint Eastwood. As both an actor and as a director, Eastwood has always been known as a tough guy. But Jolie saw a different side of him. She said that even taking into account her role as Mariane Pearl, the role of Christine Collins was her toughest challenge.

She said, "As a mother, it was harder for me imagining that someone was abusing my child while they were wondering why mommy wasn't coming to save them. As a mother, that's just the worst possible scenario. So this film was very, very painful."[16]

When a reporter asked her what got her through the toughest scenes, she gave a surprising answer. "Clint Eastwood," she replied. "There have been so many times I've worked on films that required a lot of emotion, and the director didn't understand. They'd do ten takes in a wide shot and you're crying and crying. And then they'd do close-ups and you're still trying to emote with the same honesty. Clint doesn't exhaust you like that. He knows when to move on."[17]

In February 2008, Jolie made a second goodwill trip to Iraq. Then, in mid-May she took a trip to Cannes, France. Cannes is the site of a famous film festival. Many of the world's best directors and actors are there. Jolie's costar from *Kung Fu Panda,* comedy actor Jack Black, accidentally blurted to a reporter that Jolie and Pitt were expecting twins. The media went ballistic and tried getting every detail from Jolie or Pitt. Jolie admitted it was true but was shy about giving out other details.

Black apologized and said he felt guilty about letting the news out.[18] Jolie said she had no hard feelings toward Black.[19] On July 12, 2008, Jolie gave birth to a boy and girl in Nice, France, not far from Cannes. The boy was named Knox Leon, and the girl Vivienne Marcheline. Pitt and Jolie decided to have their children in France because they have lived there and French is their family's "second language."[20]

It was also reported around that time that Jolie and her father were trying to make up. She admitted, "We have spoken recently. . . . We are going to try to get to know each other and maybe try not to be this daddy and daughter, but to be there for each other as friends in the coming years."[21]

Jolie made a goodwill trip to Afghanistan on October 24 and 25. At the same time, *Changeling* debuted in American theaters. When a megastar such as Jolie and a legend like Eastwood team up for a movie, there is bound to be a lot of excitement. Curiosity about the film was high. Most critics liked it, especially Jolie's performance. Movie critic Stephen Whitty of the Newark *Star-Ledger* was typical when he wrote about Jolie, "This is one movie where the star really is the star. And [Jolie] delivers a performance of which any actress can be truly proud."[22] Jolie was nominated for both a Golden Globe and an Academy Award for best actress, but won neither.

Like *A Mighty Heart, Changeling* did not make back the cost to produce it in United States theaters. However, between foreign showings and DVD sales and rentals, it did make a big profit.[23]

By the end of 2008, Jolie ranked as the movie industry's highest-paid female actor. She was earning on average more than $15 million per movie.[24] But with all the goodwill trips she made, and all the money she donated, nobody could say she was selfish with her earnings.

And nobody could say she did not have a sense of humor. True, she did not like jokes about humanitarians being insincere. However, former *Tonight Show* host Jay Leno featured a regular guest named Ross Matthews, also known as Ross The Intern. Ross actually once was an intern on the show. Leno turned him into a gag reporter who was often sent to pretend to cover events where celebrities appear. On January 11, 2009, Ross did interviews at the Golden Globe Awards in Los Angeles. When Jolie and Pitt walked past him, Ross called out for Jolie to please adopt him. Jolie turned back to look at Ross, then cracked up laughing.

The next month Jolie made another goodwill trip. This one was to Thailand. She found it frustrating that thousands of refugees from Myanmar were still living in enclosed camps in northern Thailand. Jolie stated, "I was saddened to meet a 21-year-old woman who was born in a refugee camp, who has never even been out of the

Jolie holds her daughter, Zahara, while Brad Pitt carries Maddox on his shoulders near the Gateway of India in Mumbai on November 12, 2006. Jolie was in India shooting *A Mighty Heart*.

camp and is now raising her own child in a camp."[25] Knowing that there was hardly any chance they would return to dangerous Myanmar soon, she said "we must find some way to help them work and become self reliant."[26] She openly called on the Thai government to give the refugees greater freedoms.

Jolie commemorated World Refugee Day, June 20, 2009, by making a thirty-second video to draw attention to the plight of refugees across the globe. The video was played on TV during the week leading up to June 20. It includes photographs and videotape footage of refugees in different locations. Jolie's video was played on television stations and on terminals in the world's airports. In the video she says, "Refugees are the most vulnerable people on earth. Every day they are fighting to survive. They deserve our respect."[27] The same week the Jolie-Pitt Foundation donated $1 million to UNHCR to help refugees living in Pakistan.[28]

> **"Refugees are the most vulnerable people on earth. Every day they are fighting to survive."**

Then, on July 23, in the heat of the desert summer, she made a third trip to Iraq to visit with refugees from the Iraq war. One man living in a basic brick shelter with his wife and six children told Jolie, "The only help we got was from UNHCR. They are the only people who knocked on our door. But look at this life, it's very hard on us." Jolie responded to him, "It takes a lot of strength for you to survive this life. I don't know if I would be strong enough to survive this."[29]

Jolie also spent much of 2009 making her next movie, *Salt*. It is a spy thriller in which Jolie plays Evelyn Salt, a CIA agent falsely accused of being a Russian spy.

Jolie has no problem keeping busy. She said, "It's hard, and maybe one day we'll have to stay in one place. . . . I'm sure [the kids are] going to be 18 and say, 'God, I just want to stay in one place.' They'll never want to leave home."[30]

Until that day, one can expect to find Angelina Jolie and her family in any country in the world, either making a movie or working for the well-being of others.

Chronology

1975— Angelina Jolie is born June 4 in Los Angeles, California to Marcheline Bertrand and actor Jon Voight; Voight leaves family soon after.

1978— Bertrand and Voight divorce; Bertrand and her children move to Palisades, New York.

1982— Has bit part with father in movie *Lookin' to Get Out*.

1986— Moves with family to Beverly Hills, California; enrolls in Lee Strasberg Theater Institute.

1989— Drops out of Beverly Hills High School briefly.

1990— Returns to Beverly Hills High School.

1991— Graduates from high school early, at age sixteen; gets modeling jobs; appears in first MTV video.

1992— Has first major role in a feature film, *Cyborg 2: Glass Shadow* (released in 1993).

1995— Has roles in the movies *Without Evidence* and *Hackers*.

1996— Marries British actor Jonny Lee Miller in March; appears in movies *Mojave Moon*, *Love Is All There Is*, and *Foxfire*.

1997— Appears in movie *Playing God;* has major roles in made-for-television movies *True Women* and *George Wallace.*

1998— Receives nominations for Golden Globe and Emmy for *George Wallace;* wins Golden Globe; stars in made-for-television movie *Gia;* acts in movies *Hell's Kitchen* and *Playing by Heart;* moves briefly to New York to study film writing and directing.

1999— Featured in movies *Pushing Tin, The Bone Collector,* and *Girl, Interrupted.*

2000— Divorces Jonny Lee Miller in April 2000; marries actor Billy Bob Thornton on May 5; is nominated for both Golden Globe and Oscar for *Girl, Interrupted* and wins both; acts in movie *Gone in 60 Seconds;* first becomes aware of harsh living conditions of refugees while filming *Lara Croft: Tomb Raider* (released in 2001) in Cambodia; contacts the United Nations to ask how to help, and is assigned to make goodwill trips for United Nations High Commissioner for Refugees (UNHCR).

2001— Stars in *Original Sin;* makes first goodwill trips for UNHCR to Sierra Leone (February), Cambodia (June and July), and Pakistan (August); in November, she and Thornton adopt a Cambodian infant they name Maddox.

Chronology

2002— Appears in one movie, *Life or Something Like It*; makes more goodwill trips for the UNHCR to Namibia (March), Thailand (May), Ecuador (June), Kenya (October), and Kosovo (December); public rift with father happens in August.

2003— Makes five more goodwill trips to Tanzania (March), Sri Lanka (April) Russia (August), Jordan (December), and Egypt (December); movies *Lara Croft Tomb Raider: The Cradle of Life* and *Beyond Borders*, based loosely on her humanitarian trips, are released; her journals from trips for UNHCR are released as the book *Notes From My Travels*; divorces Thornton on May 27; receives Citizen of the World Award from UN Correspondents' Association on October 23.

2004— Does voice-over in animated feature *Shark Tale*, and acts in the live-action movies *Taking Lives, Sky Captain and the World of Tomorrow, The Fever*, and *Alexander*; takes goodwill trips to Arizona (April), Chad (June), Thailand (October), Sudan (October), and Lebanon (December).

2005— Adopts Ethiopian child on July 6 and names her Zahara Marley Jolie; takes goodwill trips to Pakistan in May and November; costars in *Mr. and Mrs. Smith* with Brad Pitt, and they begin dating; receives the United Nations Global Humanitarian Action Award on October 11.

2006— Gives birth to daughter, Shiloh Nouvel Jolie-Pitt, on May 27; is featured in movie *The Good Shepherd*; takes goodwill trips to India (November) and Costa Rica (December); goes through tense period filming *A Mighty Heart*.

2007— Mother Marcheline Bertrand dies on January 27; takes goodwill trips to Chad (February) and Iraq and Syria (August); adopts with Pitt three-year-old boy whom they name Pax Thien Jolie-Pitt from Vietnamese orphanage in March; *A Mighty Heart* receives rave reviews but no awards; appears in movie *Beowulf*; begins intense work on next movie *Changeling*.

2008— Takes goodwill trips to Iraq (February) and Afghanistan (October); gives birth to twins (Knox Leon and Vivienne Marcheline) on July 12; begins mending relationship with father; *Wanted* is released; *Changeling* is released in fall to outstanding reviews; Jolie is nominated for both Golden Globe and Oscar awards, but wins neither.

2009— Takes goodwill trips to Thailand (February) and Iraq (July); makes videotape publicizing plight of world's refugees (June).

2010— Movie *Salt* is released.

Filmography

Goodwill Trips

February **2001**	Sierra Leone	October **2004**	Thailand, Sudan
June–July **2001**	Cambodia		
August **2001**	Pakistan	December **2004**	Lebanon
March **2002**	Namibia	May **2005**	Pakistan
May **2002**	Thailand	November **2005**	Pakistan
June **2002**	Ecuador	November **2006**	India
October **2002**	Kenya	December **2006**	Costa Rica
December **2002**	Kosovo		
March **2003**	Tanzania	February **2007**	Chad
April **2003**	Sri Lanka	August **2007**	Syria, Iraq
August **2003**	Russia	February **2008**	Iraq
December **2003**	Jordan, Egypt	October **2008**	Afghanistan
April **2004**	Arizona	February **2009**	Thailand
June **2004**	Chad	July **2009**	Iraq

Chapter Notes

Chapter 1
Land Mines and Lara Croft

1. *Angelina Jolie*, DVD, produced by Caroline Christopher (ABC News Productions for A&E Network, 2005).
2. Jenny Lange, "An Interview With Angelina Jolie," *UNHCR*, October 21, 2002, <http://www.unhcr.org/news/NEWS/3db3f99b5.html> (September 15, 2008).
3. Angelina Jolie, *Notes From My Travels* (New York: Pocket Books, 2003), p. 4.
4. Chris Connelly, "Angelina Jolie Sets the Record Straight," *Marie Claire*, July 2005, <http://www.ebscohost.com/> (September 15, 2008).

Chapter 2
"Come On, Angie, Give Us a Show!"

1. Kevin Sessums, "Wild at Heart," *Allure*, November 2004, SoulieJolie.com, n.d., <http://www.souliejolie.com/trans_article.php?id=3> (September 15, 2008).
2. "Angie Overdoes the Bad Girl Act," *Telegraph.co.uk*, October 2, 2001, <http://www.telegraph.co.uk/health/main.jhtml?xml=/health/2001/10/02/fmjoli02.xml> (September 15, 2008).
3. Lauri Sandell, "Reckless Angel: Angelina Jolie," *Biography*, October 1999, <http://www.ebscohost.com/> (September 9, 2009).
4. Rhona Mercer, *Angelina Jolie: The Biography* (London: John Blake Publishing, Ltd., 2007), p. 21.
5. Rich Cohen, "A Woman in Full," *Vanity Fair*, July 2008, p. 133.
6. Mercer, p. 4.
7. *Angelina Jolie*, DVD, produced by Caroline Christopher (ABC News Productions for A&E Network, 2005).
8. Ibid.

9. Richard Corliss, "Lookin' To Get Out," *Time*, October 18, 1982, <http://www.time.com/time/magazine/article/0,9171,949610,00.html> (October 21, 2008).

10. Sandell.

11. Rebecca Timlin-Scalera, "Angelina Jolie: What You Never Knew . . . Until Now!" *Cosmopolitan*, July 2004, <http://www.ebscohost.com/> (September 9, 2008).

Chapter 3

Cyborgs and Computer Hackers

1. Rhona Mercer, *Angelina Jolie: The Biography* (London: John Blake Publishing, Ltd., 2007), p. 11.

2. Ibid.

3. *Paula Zahn Now*, CNN transcript, June 9, 2005, <http://transcripts.cnn.com/TRANSCRIPTS/0506/09/pzn.01.html> (September 15, 2008).

4. Nancy Jo Sales, "Sex and the Single Mom," *Vanity Fair*, June 2005, <http://www.ebscohost.com/> (September 22, 2008).

5. Chris Heath, "Blood, Sugar, Sex, Magic," *Rolling Stone*, July 5, 2001, <http://www.rollingstone.com/news/story/5938014/blood_sugar_sex_magic> (September 15, 2008).

6. Mercer, p. 15.

7. Chris Connelly, "Angelina Jolie Sets the Record Straight," *Marie Claire*, July 2005, <http://www.ebscohost.com/> (September 15, 2008).

8. Mercer, p. 24.

9. Ibid., p. 26.

10. "Jonny Lee Miller and Angelina Jolie—The Happy Couple," *Empire Magazine*, June 1996, JonnyLeeMiller.co.uk, <http://www.jonnyleemiller.co.uk/angelinajolie.html> (September 6, 2008).

11. Roger Ebert, Cyborg movie review, *Chicago Sun Times*, April 7, 1989, <http://rogerebert.suntimes.com/apps/pbcs.dll/article?AID=/19890407/REVIEWS/904070301/1023> (October 30, 2008).

12. Heath.

13. Lauri Sandell, "Reckless Angel: Angelina Jolie," *Biography*, October 1999, <http://www.ebscohost.com/> (September 9, 2009).

Chapter Notes

Chapter 4

Award-Winning Angie

1. David Kronke, "Hackers," *Los Angeles Times*, September 15, 1995, <http://www.calendarlive.com/movies/reviews/cl-movie960 406-117,0,374634.story> (November 3, 2008).

2. Hal Hinson, "Hackers," *Washington Post*, September 15, 1995, <http://www.washingtonpost.com/wp-srv/style/longterm/ movies/videos/ hackersrhinson_c02d40.htm> (November 3, 2008).

3. Roger Ebert, movie review, *Chicago Sun Times*, September 15, 1995, <http://rogerebert.suntimes.com/apps/pbcs.dll/article?AID=/ 19950915/REVIEWS/509150302/1023> (November 3, 2008).

4. Ibid.

5. Joe Leydon, *Hackers* movie review, *Variety*, September 11, 1995, <http://www.variety.com/review/VE1117904423.html? categoryid=31&cs=1&query=%22Hackers%22+%22Joe+ Leydon%22> (November 3, 2008).

6. Rhona Mercer, *Angelina Jolie: The Biography* (London: John Blake Publishing, Ltd., 2007), p. 42.

7. Ibid.

8. Edward Guthmann, "Film Review—Duchovny Hurt 'Playing God'," *San Francisco Chronicle*, October 17, 1997, <http://www. sfgate.com/cgi-bin/article.cgi?f=/c/a/1997/10/17/DD35826.DTL> (November 6, 2008).

9. Liam Lacey, "Film Review," *The Globe and Mail*, October 17, 1997, <http://www.theglobeandmail.com/servlet/ArticleNews/ movie/MOVIEREVIEWS/19971017/TAGODD> (November 6, 2008).

10. "Angelina Jolie," *Turner Classic Movies*, 2009, <http://www.tcm .com/tcmdb/participant.jsp?participantId=96180|0&afiPersonal NameId=null> (November 5, 2008).

11. Janet Mock, ed., "Celebrity Central: Angelina Jolie," *People*, September 1, 2009, <http://www.people.com/people/angelina_jolie/ biography> (September 2, 2009).

12. Ibid.

13. James Berardinelli, *Playing by Heart* movie review, *Reelviews*, 1999, <http://www.reelviews.net/movies/p/playing.html> (November 10, 2008).

14. "Jonny Lee Miller XS Interview," *Sunday Mail*, October 24, 1999, *JonnyLeeMiller.co.uk*, n.d., <http://www.jonnyleemiller.co.uk/jlmxs.html> (November 3, 2008).

15. Lauri Sandell, "Reckless Angel: Angelina Jolie," *Biography*, October 1999, <http://www.ebscohost.com/> (September 9, 2009).

16. Ibid.

Chapter 5

Winning the Big One

1. Tiffany Rose, "Billy Bob Thornton: Acting Very Strange," *Independent*, September 3, 2004, <http://www.independent.co.uk/arts-entertainment/films/features/billy-bob-thornton-acting-very-strange-550994.html> (November 11, 2008).

2. Chris Heath, "Blood, Sugar, Sex, Magic," *Rolling Stone*, July 5, 2001, <http://www.rollingstone.com/news/story/5938014/blood_sugar_sex_magic> (September 15, 2008).

3. Ibid.

4. Ibid.

5. Leonard Maltin, *Leonard Maltin's 2009 Movie Guide* (New York: Signet Books, 2008), p. 1113.

6. *"The Bone Collector,"* Box Office Mojo, n.d., <http://www.boxofficemojo.com/movies/?id=bonecollector.htm> (April 6, 2009).

7. *Angelina Jolie*, DVD, produced by Caroline Christopher (ABC News Productions for A&E Network, 2005).

8. Kenneth Turan, *Girl, Interrupted* movie review, *Los Angeles Times*, December 21, 1999, <http://www.calendarlive.com/movies/reviews/cl-movie000406-84,0,1294435.story> (November 12, 2008).

9. Peter Stack, "Sappy 'Girl' Lacks Sufficient Power," *San Francisco Chronicle*, n.d., <http://www.sfgate.com/cgi-bin/article.cgi?f=/c/a/2000/06/09/DD39773.DTL> (November 12, 2008).

10. Jack Garner, *Girl, Interrupted* movie review, *Rochester Democrat and Chronicle*, January 14, 2000, <http://www.rochestergoesout.com/mov/g/girlin.html> (November 12, 2008).

11. *Girl, Interrupted*, DVD, directed by James Mangold (Sony Pictures, 2000).

12. Dave Carger, "Angelina Jolie: A Candid Q&A," *Entertainment Weekly*, June 11, 2008, <http://www.ew.com/ew/article/0,,20205854,00.html> (November 1, 2008).

13. "Early to Wed," *People*, May 22, 2000, <http://www.ebscohost
    .com/> (November 3, 2008).

14. Ibid.

15. *Gone in Sixty Seconds* movie review, *Variety*, June 8, 2000, <http://
    www.variety.com/review/VE1117787317.html?categoryid=31
    &cs=1> (April 6, 2009).

16. Eugene Novikov, *Gone in Sixty Seconds* movie review, *Film Blather*,
    2000, <http://www.filmblather.com/review.php?n=gonein60
    seconds> (April 6, 2009).

17. *"Gone in 60 Seconds," Box Office Mojo*, n.d., <http://www.box
    officemojo.com/movies/?id=gonein60seconds.htm> (April 6, 2009).

18. *"Lara Croft: Tomb Raider," Box Office Mojo*, n.d., <http://www.
    boxofficemojo.com/movies/?id=tombraider.htm> (April 6, 2009).

19. "Crafting Lara Croft," *Lara Croft: Tomb Raider*, DVD, directed by
    Simon West (Hollywood: Paramount Pictures, 2001).

20. Ibid.

21. Ibid.

22. Jack Garner, *Lara Croft: Tomb Raider* movie review, *Rochester
    Democrat and Chronicle*, June 15, 2001, <http://www.rochester
    goesout.com/mov/l/laracr.html> (April 6, 2009).

23. *Angelina Jolie* DVD.

Chapter 6

Sleeping With the Spiders

1. Angelina Jolie, *Notes From My Travels* (New York: Pocket Books,
   2003), pp. 26–27.

2. Ibid., p. 27.

3. Ibid., p. 79.

4. Jenny Lange, "An Interview With Angelina Jolie," *UNHCR*,
   October 21, 2002, <http://www.unhcr.org/news/NEWS/3db3f
   99b5.html> (September 15, 2008).

5. Ibid.

6. Jolie, p. 103.

7. *"Original Sin," Box Office Mojo*, n.d., <http://www.boxoffice
   mojo.com/movies/?id=originalsin.htm> (April 6, 2009).

8. Rebecca Timlin-Scalera, "Angelina Jolie: What You Never Knew
   . . . Until Now!" *Cosmopolitan*, July 2004, <http://www.ebsco
   host.com/> (September 9, 2008).

9. Jolie, p. 166.

10. Ibid., p. 167

11. Ibid., p. 191.

12. *Angelina Jolie*, DVD, produced by Caroline Christopher (ABC News Productions for A&E Network, 2005).

Chapter 7

"Don't Go Off the Path"

1. Mick LaSalle, "Jolie and Burns give 'Life' to Drama," *San Francisco Chronicle*, April 26, 2002, <http://www.sfgate.com/cgi-bin/article.cgi?f=/c/a/2002/04/26/DD59963.DTL> (December 2, 2008).

2. Angelina Jolie, *Notes From My Travels* (New York: Pocket Books, 2003), p. 196.

3. "Goodwill Ambassador Angelina Jolie Ends Ecuador Mission," *UNHCR*, June 10, 2002, <http://www.unhcr.org/news/NEWS/3d04d46e4.html> (September 15, 2008).

4. Ibid.

5. Rhona Mercer, *Angelina Jolie: The Biography* (London: John Blake Publishing, Ltd., 2007), p. 188.

6. Ibid.

7. Gary Susman, "Null and Voight," *Entertainment Weekly*, August 2, 2002, <http://www.ew.com/ew/article/0,,333476,00.html> (November 11, 2008).

8. Ibid.

9. Ibid.

10. Mercer, p. 191.

11. Ibid.

12. Susman.

13. Ibid.

14. "Angelina Jolie's Kosovo Journal," *UNHCR*, December 24, 2002, <http://www.unhcr.org/news/joliekosovo.pdf> (December 3, 2008).

15. Ibid.

16. Bruce Kirkland, "The New Angelina Jolie," *Sun*, October 19, 2003, <http://jam.canoe.ca/Movies/Artists/J/Jolie_Angelina/2003/10/19/759420.html> (September 15, 2008).

17. "Angelina Jolie's Sri Lanka Journal," *UNHCR*, April14–15, 2003, <http://www.unhcr.org/news/joliesri-lanka.pdf> (December 3, 2008).

18. Ibid.

19. "'I No Longer See Us as Father and Daughter'—Angelina Jolie," *BBC Press Office*, September 8, 2003, <http://www.bbc.co.uk/press office/bbcworldwide/worldwidestories/pressreleases/2003/08_ august/angelia_jolie.shtml> (September 12, 2008).

20. Daniel M. Kimmel, "The New Lara Croft Has No Reason to Exist Except That the First One Made Money," *Worcester Telegram and Gazette*, January 2, 2004, Rottentomatoes.com, n.d., <http://www.rottentomatoes.com/m/lara_croft_tomb_raider_the_cradle_ of_life/articles/1234380/the_new_lara_croft_has_no_reason_to_ exist_except_that_the_first_one_made_money> (December 13, 2008).

21. *"Lara Croft Tomb Raider: The Cradle of Life,"* Box Office Mojo, n.d., <http://www.boxofficemojo.com/movies/?id=tombraider2.htm> (April 7, 2009).

22. "Angelina Jolie's Russian Journal," *UNHCR*, August 19–24, 2003, <http://www.unhcr.org/news/jolierussia.pdf> (December 13, 2008).

23. Ibid.

24. Ibid.

25. Ibid.

26. Ibid.

27. Ibid.

28. *"Beyond Borders," Box Office Mojo*, n.d., <http://www.boxoffice mojo.com/movies/?id=beyondborders.htm> (December 13, 2008).

29. James Berardinelli, *Beyond Borders* movie review, *Reelviews*, 2003, <http://www.reelviews.net/movies/b/beyond_borders.html> (December 13, 2008).

30. Jolie, x.

31. "Jolie Wins Award for UN Work," *BBC News*, October 24, 2003, <http://news.bbc.co.uk/2/hi/entertainment/3210987.stm> (September 12, 2008).

Chapter 8

Darfur and the Janjaweed

1. "Jolie Gives Hospital £50,000," *BBC News World Edition*, November 25, 2002, <http://news.bbc.co.uk/2/hi/uk_news/england/ 2510491.stm> (September 12, 2008).

2. Ibid.

3. Nancy Jo Sales, "Sex and the Single Mom," *Vanity Fair*, June 2005, <http://www.ebscohost.com/> (September 22, 2008).

4. Ibid.

5. Jonathan Van Meter, "Learning to Fly," *Vogue*, March 2004, *Style.com*, 2007, <http://www.ebscohost.com/> (September 15, 2008).

6. Ibid.

7. "Jolie's Jordan Journal Gives Voice to the Displaced and Desperate," *UNHCR*, March 15, 2004, <http://www.unhcr.org/cgi-bin/texis/vtx/search?page=search&docid=40557fb34&query=angelina jolie journal> (March 22, 2009).

8. "Angelina Jolie's Jordan Journal," *UNHCR*, December 10, 2003, p. 3, <http://www.unhcr.org/4a07ee4a6.html> (September 3, 2009).

9. Van Meter.

10. Lilli Tnaib, "UNHCR Goodwill Ambassador Angelina Jolie Launches Centre for Unaccompanied Children," *UNHCR*, March 9, 2007, <http://www.unhcr.org/news/NEWS/422f33944.html> (September 15, 2008).

11. "Goodwill Ambassador Jolie Visits Detained Children in Arizona," *UNHCR*, April 29, 2004, <http://www.unhcr.org/news/NEWS/4090d9147.html> (March 23, 2009).

12. Ibid.

13. "Jolie Laments Children's Plight in Darfur, Calls for More Security," *UNHCR*, October 27, 2004, <http://www.unhcr.org/news/NEWS/417fce4e4.html> (March 23, 2009).

14. "Urgent Funds Needed for Darfur Refugees, Stresses Jolie," *UNHCR*, June 7, 2004, <http://www.unhcr.org/news/NEWS/40c4694f4.html> (March 23, 2009).

15. "Jolie Laments Children's Plight in Darfur."

16. "Angelina Jolie—An Actor on a Mission," *BBC News Front Page*, December 20, 2004, <http://news.bbc.co.uk/2/hi/programmes/hardtalk/4098423.stm> (September 12, 2008).

17. Fred Schruers, "Angelina Jolie," *Premiere*, October 2004, <http://www.ebscohost.com/> (September 15, 2008).

18. Rhona Mercer, *Angelina Jolie: The Biography* (London: John Blake Publishing, Ltd., 2007), p. 214.

19. Rick Groen, "Alexander? No So Great," *The Globe and Mail*, November 24, 2004, <http://www.theglobeandmail.com/servlet/ArticleNews/movie/MOVIEREVIEWS/20041124/ALEXANDER 24> (March 24, 2009).

20. Andrew Sarris, "Alexander's Not So Great-Stone's Horny Hero Is a Bore," *New York Observer*, November 28, 2004, <http://www.observer.com/node/50125> (March 24, 2009).
21. Ty Burr, "'Sky Captain' Soars Back to Classic Sci-fi Worlds With Gleaming Digital Technology," *Boston Globe*, September 18, 2004, <http://www.boston.com/movies/display?display=movie&id=5692> (March 24, 2009).
22. Ibid.

Chapter 9

Mr. and Mrs. Smith Fall in Love

1. Rhona Mercer, *Angelina Jolie: The Biography* (London: John Blake Publishing, Ltd., 2007), pp. 233–234.
2. Ibid., p. 239.
3. Jack Redden, "Afghan Repatriation From Pakistan Exceeds 50,000 as Jolie Visits," *UNHCR*, May 6, 2005, <http://www.unhcr.org/news/NEWS/427b69ce4.html> (March 24, 2009).
4. Ibid.
5. Michelle Tauber, "Angelina Adopts a Girl: And Baby Makes Three," *People*, July 18, 2005, <http://www.people.com/people/archive/article/0,,20148166,00.html> (September 10, 2008).
6. Ibid.
7. Chris Strauss, "Zahara's Fight," *People*, August 1, 2005, <http://www.people.com/people/archive/article/0,,20143949,00.html> (September 10, 2008).
8. Ibid.
9. "Jolie Given Cambodian Citizenship," *BBC News Front Page*, August 12, 2005, <http://news.bbc.co.uk/2/hi/entertainment/4144518.stm> (September 15, 2008).
10. Ibid.
11. "Jolie Honored for Refugee Role," *BBC News Front Page*, October 12, 2005, <http://news.bbc.co.uk/2/hi/entertainment/4333544.stm> (September 15, 2008).
12. Jack Redden, "Goodwill Ambassador Jolie Sees Urgency of More Aid in Pakistan," *UNHCR*, November 28, 2005, <http://unhcr.org/news/NEWS/438ae6ab14.html> (March 24, 2009).
13. Ibid.
14. Mercer, p. 262.

15. Karen Thomas, "Charity Follows Shiloh," *USA Today*, May 30, 2006, <http://www.ebscohost.com/> (September 11, 2008).

16. Mercer, p. 265.

17. Thomas.

18. Mercer, p. 267.

19. Michelle Tauber, "New Baby, New Lives," *People*, January 30, 2006, <http://www.people.com/people/archive/article/0,,20156685,00 .html> (September 10, 2008).

20. Ann Curry, "Angelina Jolie on Film, Family, and the Future," *Dateline NBC*, May 23, 2007, *MSNBC.com*, May 24, 2007, <http://www.msnbc.msn.com/id/18833893/> (September 12, 2008).

21. Ibid.

22. Kitty McKinsey, "Goodwill Ambassador Angelina Jolie Applauds Courage of Refugees in India," *UNHCR*, November 6, 2006, <http://unhcr.org/news/NEWS/454f05d62.html> (March 29, 2009).

23. Ibid.

Chapter 10

"She's Absolutely Serious"

1. Matthew Swibe, "Bad Girl, Interrupted," *Forbes*, July 3, 2006, <http://www.forbes.com/forbes/2006/0703/118_print.html> (September 15, 2008).

2. Ibid.

3. Jonathan Van Meter, "Learning to Fly," *Vogue*, March 2004, *Style.com*, 2007, <http://web.archive.org/web/20071221225830/ http://www.style.com/vogue/feature/022304/page2.html> (September 15, 2008).

4. Ibid.

5. Lawrence Christon, "Angelina Jolie," *Variety*, July 30, 2007, <http:// www.variety.com/article/VR1117969270.html?categoryid= 2160&cs=1&query=Angelina+Jolie&query=Angelina+Jolie> (August 31, 2009).

6. Mary Green, "Angelina's Heartbreak," *People*, February 12, 2007, <http://www.people.com/people/article/0,,20010291,00.html> (September 10, 2008).

7. Angelina Jolie, "Justice for Darfur," *Washington Post*, February 28, 2007, <http://www.washingtonpost.com/wp-dyn/content/article/2007/02/27/AR2007022701161.html> (March 23, 2009).

8. Ibid.

9. Ibid.

10. "Angelina Jolie Adopts Vietnam Boy," *BBC News Front Page*, March 15, 2007, <http://news.bbc.co.uk/2/hi/entertainment/6452741.stm> (September 15, 2008).

11. "Angelina Jolie Commits to World's Children," *MSNBC.com*, May 4, 2007, <http://www.msnbc.msn.com/id/18425828> (September 12, 2008).

12. "Mission Statement," *Maddox-Jolie Pitt Foundation*, 2007–2009, <http://www.mjpasia.org/mission.htm> (April 11, 2009).

13. "Critics Praise Angelina Jolie's 'Mighty' Role," *MSNBC.com*, May 22, 2007, <http://www.msnbc.msn.com/id/18809101> (September 12, 2008).

14. Roger Ebert, *A Mighty Heart* movie review, *Chicago Sun-Times*, June 22, 2007, <http://rogerebert.suntimes.com/apps/pbcs.dll/article?AID=/20070621/REVIEWS/70621002/1023> (March 31, 2009).

15. *"A Mighty Heart,"* Box Office Mojo, n.d., <http://www.boxofficemojo.com/movies/?id=mightyheart.htm> (March 31, 2009).

16. Jeanne Wolf, "Angelina Jolie: My Painful Role," *Parade*, October 9, 2008, <http://www.parade.com/celebrity/celebrity-parade/archive/angelina-jolie-changeling.html> (October 13, 2008).

17. Ibid.

18. Brooke Anderson, "Behind the Scenes: Jolie Takes Uproar in Stride," *CNN.com*, May 16, 2008, <http://www.cnn.com/2008/SHOWBIZ/Movies/05/16/bts.cannes.anderson/index.html?iref=newssearch> (September 12, 2008).

19. Ibid.

20. Michelle Tauber, "And Babies Make Eight," *People*, July 27, 2008, <http://www.ebscohost.com/> (September 10, 2008).

21. Rennie Dyball, "Speaking to Her Dad Again," *People*, June 16, 2008, <http://www.people.com/people/archive/article/0,,20207264,00.html> (August 31, 2009).

22. Stephen Whitty, "The Mother of All Devoted Moms," (Newark) *Star-Ledger*, October 23, 3008, <http://www.nj.com/entertainment/tv/index.ssf/2008/10/the_mother_of_all_devoted_moms.html> (March 31, 2009).

23. *"Changeling," Box Office Mojo*, n.d., <http://www.boxofficemojo
    .com/movies/?id=changeling08.htm> (March 31, 2009).

24. Associated Press, "Winfrey, Jolie Hollywood No. 1s," *Keene* (New
    Hampshire) *Sentinel*, December 6, 2008, p. 8.

25. Kitty McKinsey, "Angelina Jolie Voices Support for Myanmar
    Refugees in Northern Thailand Camp," *UNHCR*, February 5,
    2009, <http://www.unhcr.org/news/NEWS/498ab65c2.html>
    (March 31, 2009).

26. Ibid.

27. "Angelina Jolie Releases New Video to Draw Attention to Plight of
    Refugees Around the World," *UNHCR*, June 16, 2009, <http://
    www.unhcr.org/cgi-bin/texis/vtx/search?page=search&docid=
    4a37a0466&query=angelina%20jolie%20video> (July 31, 2009).

28. "UN Refugee Agency Receives $1 Million From Jolie-Pitt Founda-
    tion for Displaced Families in Pakistan," *UNHCR*, June 17, 2009,
    <http://www.unhcr.org/cgi-bin/texis/vtx/search?page=
    search&docid=4a41dd999&query=jolie%20pitt%20foundation>
    (July 31, 2009).

29. "Angelina Jolie Pays Third Visit to Iraq, Appeals for Aid for the Dis-
    placed," *UNHCR*, July 23, 2009, <http://www.unhcr.org/cgi-bin/
    texis/vtx/search?page=search&docid=4a687fa29&query=
    angelina%20jolie%20iraq> (July 31, 2009).

30. Mary Green, "Angelina Jolie Talks About Life, Love and Family,"
    People, December 13, 2006, <http://www.people.com/people/
    article/0,,20004172,00.html> (November 3, 2008).

Further Reading

Books

Bjornlund, Lydia. *Angelina Jolie.* Philadelphia, Pa.: Mason Crest Pub., 2009.

Jolie, Angelina. *Notes From My Travels.* New York: Pocket Books, 2003.

LaBella, Laura. *Angelina Jolie: Goodwill Ambassador for the United Nations.* New York: Rosen Publishing Group, 2008.

Lynette, Rachel. *Angelina Jolie.* San Diego, Calif.: Lucent Books, 2006.

Tracy Kathleen. *Angelina Jolie: A Biography.* Westport, CT: Greenwood Press, 2009.

Internet Sites

Angelina Jolie Web site
http://www.angelinajolieweb.org/

Maddox Jolie-Pitt Foundation (MJP)
http://www.mjpasia.org/

The United Nations Refugee Agency (UNHCR)
http://www.unhcr.org/cgi-bin/texis/vtx/home

Index

Index